BEYOND TEARS

IRMGARD LITTEN

BEYOND TEARS

by

IRMGARD LITTEN

Introduction and Epilogue by
PIERRE VAN PAASSEN

Foreword by
HIS GRACE THE ARCHBISHOP OF YORK

Preface by
W. ARNOLD-FORSTER

ALLIANCE BOOK CORPORATION

NEW YORK

FOREWORD

I hope this book may be widely read as a moving human record which illustrates the spirit of the Nazi tyranny.

WILLIAM EBOR,
The Archbishop of York.

Bishop Thorpe, York
May 22, 1940.

INTRODUCTION

THIS BOOK IS the story of a son and his mother. That the son was an exceptional personality is merely incidental. That the mother, the author of this volume, is an extraordinary human being is, in the final analysis, unimportant. But that both of them fought undauntedly for their decency and integrity in a country where intellectual honesty is a crime punishable by torture and death—that is of great consequence.

To the story of Hans and Irmgard Litten nothing needs to be added. In its simplicity it transcends the individual tragedy and becomes a heroic epic, a symbol of the calvary of manhood and motherhood under Hitler.

It seemed to me that to close this book with the tragic end of Hans Litten would leave it incomplete. Litten personified the final struggle of democracy in Germany. Today, when the forces that destroyed Litten threaten to overrun the last rampart of democracy, in our own hemisphere, it is but right that the martyrdom of Irmgard Litten's son serve as a warning to the free men of this country. That is why I trace once more, as an epilogue to the Litten story, the implications which the Hitler triumph in Europe has for America.

August, 1940   PIERRE VAN PAASSEN

PREFACE

HERE IS ONE of the heroic stories of the Nazi Terror—
the story of the torture and death of Hans Litten, and of
his mother's long fight to save him.

Perhaps you feel that, in a world so full of suffering
and cruelty, you cannot bear to read another word about
such a subject. But I think you will not be sorry to have
read this brief record. You will find something of greatness, something that lightens the world, in the loving
steadfastness and the amazing courage of the frail elderly
woman, Frau Litten, who found in herself the strength
to sustain the long struggle here recounted. And the
man whose endurance and agony is indicated here—it
can never be described—was no ordinary man. He died
upholding a principle of law which is of fundamental importance. Some day, when the German people shake off
the Nazi tyranny and return to some kind of partnership
in Western civilization, the name of Hans Litten will be
among those which a liberal Germany will honour. May
this book serve as part of his memorial.

As a record of Frau Litten's struggle to save her son's
life, the book speaks for itself. But a brief introduction
may be acceptable for English and American readers, to

explain the conditions in which Litten had to work, what was the work he did, and how he incurred Hitler's special hatred.

In 1929, when the young lawyer, Hans Litten, first became prominent, Germany was already sickening with the disease of Nazism. Hitler was receiving financial backing from wealthy capitalists who desired, as he did, to smash the weakly democratic regime of Weimar and Stresemann's policy of "fulfilment."

Under this stimulus, murders and street fighting became very frequent. Socialists and Communists were driven to adopt similar measures. And as the menace of Nazi power grew, law in Germany became weaker and weaker as an objective guardian of justice. Judges began to lose their standards of impartiality and lawyers their standards of professional honour. Corruption was setting in.

A picture of young Litten, beginning his career as a lawyer under these conditions, is given by Dr. Rudolf Olden in an introduction to the German edition of this book.

"He was a Franciscan character," says Olden; and one can discern something of this in Litten's portrait—the small, round head, cropped in prison style, and the bright fearless eyes behind the circles of his glasses. "He might conceivably have lived through the republican era un-scathed, might have lived to be a citizen of the Third Reich, had not his profession made him the protagonist of justice. Inevitably, he came into conflict with those who were climbing to power by breaking the law, and also with the official guardians of the law when once these began to tolerate the law-breaker and to frown upon those who fought for justice. For the sake of jus-tice he suffered imprisonment, torture, and death."

In May 1931 Litten found himself up against the Prosecutor, in a case in which he was presenting claims on behalf of two workmen who were stabbed at a New Year party by Nazis of Storm Troop 33. It is worth re-calling this case in some detail, since it was this trial which specially aroused Hitler's animosity against Litten, and so led to the slow, brutal revenge described in this book.

Litten wanted to establish in court that acts of vio-lence against workers, such as those committed in this instance, were not spontaneous explosions of passion but were planned in advance, and that they were tolerated by the Nazi Party and contemplated in its programme. For Litten realized that if Hitler's conception of the totali-tarian State were to prevail, law would cease to be objec-tive, an impartial guardian of the citizen's rights, but would become an instrument of national policy, slave of a Führer's will.[1] So, at Litten's request, Hitler himself, as leader of the Nazi Party, was called as a witness and was cross-examined by Litten.

Hitler was in a dilemma. On the one hand, he wanted to allay the fears of his wealthy middle-class supporters, and of old President Hindenburg, by assurances that the Party stood only for legal, constitutional methods. He had therefore sworn an oath to this effect at an earlier trial in Leipzig.

But on the other hand, Hitler had to satisfy his gangsters; he had to convince the young bloods of the Storm Troops that all such public professions of legality were in reality a mere smoke-screen, to mask the Party's opportunist climb to power. And he had to avoid any open disavowal of his militant colleague, Goebbels.

Realizing Hitler's embarrassment, Litten drove Hitler into making more and more emphatic declarations of the

---

[1] That, of course, is exactly what did happen. In August 1932, fifteen months after the trial here referred to, the German Special Court at Beuthen condemned to death five Nazis who had been found guilty of an unspeakably brutal murder. Hitler telegraphed to the murderers: "Comrades, in the face of this murderous, bloody verdict, I feel myself united to you by bonds of unlimited loyalty. From this moment on, it is a matter of honour for us to secure your freedom. To struggle against the Government which permitted this is our duty." Hitler followed this by a manifesto from the Brown House, denouncing the "bloody objectivity" of the Government of the day, von Papen's. "In view of this monstrous, bloody verdict, we have only one thing to live for; *struggle and struggle on*. We are determined to free the conception of Nationalism from its association with an *objectivity* which in its heart of hearts is directed against National Germany, as the verdict of Beuthen shows."

Two years later the climax came, when Chancellor Hitler, after his murders on "the Night of the Long Knives," June 20, 1934, declared that he himself was then the supreme law of Germany.

strict legality of the Party's policy: wilder and wilder lies. And then he challenged Hitler to square these professions with Goebbels' notorious incitements to violence. "Did not Dr. Goebbels once declare," he asked, "that adversaries must be crushed to pulp?" "That, of course," Hitler parried, "is not to be taken literally." "Must it not exert a considerable influence in the ranks of the Party members when a man in such a position as Dr. Goebbels says this kind of thing: 'We must proceed from the revolution of words to the revolution of deeds and at the fitting moment lay violent hands on power?'" Hitler replied: "Our Party is recruited from all strata of the German people. Those who came to us from the Communist camp still have bits of the Communistic egg-shell sticking to them, and those who come to us from the bourgeois camp have bits of bourgeois egg-shell. That does not affect a man's capacity and it does not affect his desire to work for Germany's greatness and her future. The main thing is that he stands on the basis of legality. The straight line of legality must be observed by all Party officials; whoever departs from it is degraded or expelled from the Party." To this Litten retorted: "Isn't it inconsistent with this that Dr. Goebbels, despite his crass profession of illegality, is not degraded or expelled from the Party, but is on the contrary made *Gauführer* and head of the *Reichs* propaganda? This must surely give rise to the very general opinion that legality is not to be so very seriously observed?"

Hitler could only reply: "The opinion of the Party is that it stands on a legal basis!"

After two hours of cross-examination, Litten asked: "Then what do you understand by the volunteer spirit which you are expecting?" Hitler: "I understand by this, that a man shall support it not only physically but in every respect with body and soul." Litten: "Do you think you can attune this volunteer spirit to the acts of violence and the murders which are perpetrated?" At this reference to the Vehm murders committed by the Nazis, Hitler flew into a passion. "I refuse to speak of murders here. The men were defending their Fatherland."

The trial ended some weeks later, when the Nazi terrorists, belonging to Storm Troop 33, were condemned to long terms of imprisonment.

Hitler never forgave or forgot that ordeal.

This inadequate summary of one of the incidents in Litten's brief career may suffice to show that he was indeed fearless, selfless, sometimes perhaps too imprudent, in a magnificent struggle to keep justice afloat in a Germany where justice was foundering in a sea of party passion. It may serve too to show why the Nazis, and especially Hitler, hated him.

At the end of February 1933 came the Reichstag fire, followed immediately by Goering's monstrous round-up of opponents of the Nazi regime. Litten was one of those seized, and was sent to Spandau prison, without trial, charge, or sentence.

At this point Frau Litten's story begins. I need not here try to summarize it. I will only say that all the information which could be obtained in England from other sources, from December 1933 until Litten's death, confirms the story which I have now read more fully in this book. I have before me, for instance, a sworn account, by a most competent witness, of the injuries which Litten was suffering from when brought back to Spandau Prison from Sonnenburg Camp. Frau Litten's account on page 47 is perfectly accurate, but an understatement.

You will read in this book how Litten was tortured to induce him to betray the secrets of his clients. You will read of his being shifted from camp to camp, sometimes comparatively well treated, but generally the victim it seems of the Nazis' special brutality. You will see something of that "Franciscan character" shining through the mask of suffering, until death released him.

W. ARNOLD-FORSTER

Contents

CONTENTS

PART III
BUCHENWALD AND DACHAU

PART I
SONNENBURG TO ESTERWEGEN

Before the Storm

"AND NOW, my dear child, what should I wish for you? In your choice of a home you have chosen well; life will offer you much that is beautiful, and we may hope that you will become a good and a happy man." These were the words addressed by the pastor to our eldest son, Hans Achim, at his baptism, while his godfather, Franz von Liszt, the eminent criminal lawyer, held the child in his arms. We thought as the pastor thought. Why should he not look forward to a happy and prosperous life?

My husband came of a well-to-do family, and we could but assume that our wealth would assure us and our children of a care-free and comfortable existence.

My husband's family had produced prosperous merchants, able lawyers, and eminent physicians. It was therefore to be expected that he too—who a few days before the birth of our son (1903) had been incepted into the juridical faculty of the University of Halle—should have had a successful career before him. Only two years later he was appointed professor in ordinary in the University of Königsberg, and since he was happy to be in his native city he abandoned all idea of a wider career; and in a suburb of Königsberg we built a beautiful house, in which our children (for Hans was followed by two further sons) passed a sheltered and care-free childhood.

Hans Achm, with his thick fair curls and his big, rather reproachful eyes, was a striking child. I felt proud when people stopped in the street and admired "the beautiful child." I was still prouder when one day on the Baltic seashore a man of impressive appearance stood considering the two-year-old boy. "That's a wonderful head you've got, my boy!" he said. "You'll be a famous man one of these days!" I heard afterwards that the stranger was the well-known pathologist, Bernhardt Naunyn.

The boy grew very quickly; he was a model scholar, but by no means a model child; he was highly imaginative, and had the most original ideas. Besides his early and pronounced interest in science and art, he had two very marked characteristics: his great kindness and affection for poor people, and his love of animals. My old East Prussian cook often complained that "the young master" had again been behaving queerly: he had given his breakfast to the crossing-sweeper, with whom he was on terms of the closest friendship; he had addressed the beggar as "Herr," offering him, with a low bow, the food which he had taken from the pantry, whereas he never showed such respect to "the gentry" who visited the house.

Even more striking was his fanatical love of truth, his remembrance of the given word, and his absolute insistence that a promise once given must be honoured. If anyone had frivolously made him a promise that could only with difficulty be kept, Hans would never leave his side, constantly repeating, with a look of reproach: "But you promised; you must do it!" until the seemingly impossible thing was performed. In this one saw the first germ of the "Michael Kohlhaas" temper which he afterwards developed: the temper of the patient, honest, persistent German; naturally enough, for all the members of my family are afflicted with it. We have all made life difficult for ourselves by our invincible sense of justice.

The great majority of my forefathers were pastors; all, from the beginning of the seventeenth century and earlier, were Swabians; and most of them were fearless soldiers of God. One of them was so pugnacious, so extreme in his demands upon the righteousness of his flock, that the authorities, regarding him as impossible, sent him to Russia, to preach to the Germans on the Volga, where he built up a flourishing community. Hans Achim often reminded me of this ancestor, both in appearance and in character.

I was an innocent child when I married. My father was a university professor. I knew nothing of the luxuries of life; but expenditure on things of intellectual and spiritual value was taken as a matter of course in my parents' house. I had not the least notion of the realities of life; my interests were exclusively artistic and scientific. My only prominent characteristics were my fanatical love of truth and my obstinacy, which many people call "character." Both my intellectual interests and my other qualities have been inherited by my children.

It was perhaps a misfortune for them that during the years of the war—since my husband was at the front all the time—the education of the children was left entirely to me. I taught them that material interests must never be allowed to control one's actions; that one must be faithful to one's own convictions with fanatical obstinacy; that a compromise was never permissible. Since I had never come into contact with the seamy side of life I had never realized what a lifelong handicap such an attitude would be.

At the beginning of the war Hans Achim was as enthusiastic and militaristic as any other German boy. He observed all the prescribed restrictions with the utmost conscientiousness. If he happened to consider that there was more than the prescribed amount of meat or butter on the table he would stop eating. The head of the Food Ministry (Reichsernährungs-minister), Batocki, told me: "I am convinced that he is the only German who unconditionally obeys my regulations!"

After the second year of the war, Hans Achim began to think for himself. A keen observer, he noted the difference in the treatment of officers and men. We were in a position to make the comparison, for my husband went to the front as an officer, while my brothers had to win their commissions in the field. I did not bridle my tongue, and I believe what he heard and saw at this time gave him the first impetus to his socialistic and pacifist attitude.

In the inflation we, like so many Germans, lost our fortune. My husband's comment was this: "I have no intention of changing our style of living; I shall simply earn more." And he did actually earn so much, as juridical expert and arbitrator, and by writing for the Press, that we continued to live as usual.

Nevertheless, the loss of our capital had some bearing on the choice of a career for Hans Achim. We had always taken it for granted that he would be a *savant*. The subject that interested him more especially was comparative philology. But could a philologist, in the years after the war, hope for a secure livelihood? My husband, in his enthusiasm for his own profession, wished Hans to study the law. If more prosperous times should return he could always drop the law for a more scientific profession.

Hans Achim devoted himself to his legal studies with his usual conscientiousness, although at this period he gave much of his time to the Youth Movement, in which he played a leading part, working for its political establishment. He now called himself Hans Litten only; Hans Achim was "too feudal" for him.

He was from his childhood a fanatic for justice. Now,

when the practice of the law had become his profession, he recognized the serious defects in the administration of justice. In all his activities the longing to wage impassioned war for justice and righteousness became increasingly apparent. I rejoiced in this; but my husband, who knew more of life than I, was full of misgivings. My son's political and social opinions, which were now becoming more and more definite, were in absolute opposition to those of his father. My husband himself now suggested that there was still time for Hans to adopt another profession, hoping that his preference for scientific studies would make him forgetful of politics. But Hans refused to make the change. Despite his longing for a more congenial profession, he felt that it was his duty to live and fight for what he held to be right. And this he could do only in the capacity of advocate.

When Hans had passed his examinations and had qualified as assessor (assistant judge) he had several offers of posts in the Ministry of Justice. He declined them: he did not wish to bind himself by the obligations of a State functionary. He was offered a lucrative position in partnership with another advocate, which would have left him free for half the day, but this, too, he refused. When I suggested that he could live a full life on such an income, and help other people, and devote the other half of the day to cases in which he was interested, he exclaimed: "I must not waste a moment of my time." He was in the true sense of the word the advocate of the poor, of those who were outcast by the ruling social order. He belonged to no party, but there were naturally many Socialists and Communists among those whom he defended, especially when he developed his practice as defending counsel in the criminal courts. Before he had been three years in the profession his activity in this connection was attracting general attention, and he could no longer undertake all the work that was offered him. Nevertheless, he lived almost in a state of poverty; for his clients were all poor people. If they were not in receipt of assistance from benevolent or friendly societies he defended them without payment. He used to work literally day and night. And although it seems incredible, he was none the less able to acquire a quite exceptional knowledge of all branches of art, and he was able to read a great number of languages, beginning with Sanskrit.

His life was in strange contrast to our own. We lived in what for the home of a university professor was a life of luxury. In East Prussia, soon after the war, the old social life was revived, with its reactionary valuation of men according to rank and dignity, its rigid insistence on law and convention, and its formal dinners of many courses and vintage wines. Hans refused to have anything to do with such affairs. I too disliked such functions, and made fun of them, but when my husband became rector of the university I had perforce to attend them and behave myself.

There was no denying the fact that my husband was a prominent figure in East Prussia. He had a great reputation as teacher. The Crown Prince sent his eldest son to study under him. Indeed, my husband was often called in jest the "uncrowned king of East Prussia." Those who value such things would say that his was a brilliant career.

I felt more comfortable in the company of my sons. I often went to Chemnitz and Leipzig for a few days, in order to enjoy the artistic achievements of my two younger boys: Heinz was then a producer, Rainer an actor. My visits to Hans' apartments were shorter; for it was never possible to see much of him. He was on the go from early in the morning until late in the evening, and when he did spare me a few hours he always had a feeling that he was neglecting his clients. He never allowed himself a proper vacation. But we always had a great deal to say to each other, and we understood each other perfectly. I was able to help him with money. He would no longer accept an allowance from his father, as he naturally spent the money in ways of which my husband disapproved. But money never remained in his pocket for more than a few hours; there were always so many people whom he positively had to help. I am sure his kindness and generosity were greatly exploited. But his friends, and many of those whom he had helped, were ready to go through fire and water for him.

My three sons got on very well together. Although

they had the same education, they were very different from one another. Each thought the others, with their different attitude to life, a little crazy; they used to laugh at one another, and above all at the "faithful Hans," who was so generous and unworldly. But they had the most unstinted admiration for him.

My son's repeated successes in the fight against the ever-increasing blood-lust of the "brown hordes" filled me with pride and my husband with misgiving. For me, a case in which Hans was briefed was an event. He was not a man who practised his profession in order to earn his living. He was a fanatic, a man who was fearlessly fulfilling a mission.

CHAPTER II

Sonnenburg—The Stormtrooper's Revenge

ON THE NIGHT OF THE REICHSTAG fire my son was arrested. I had been worried about him since the Felseneck trial. I had begged him to go abroad, at least for a time. A house and money were placed at his disposal in a foreign country. But he repudiated all such suggestions with the words: "The millions of workers can't leave the country; I must remain here."

On the 28th of February, 1933, at four o'clock in the morning, he was roused from his bed. The arrest, it seems, was effected quite amiably; for his friends, the Fürsts, with whom he shared the apartment, told me that he took his bath more quietly and leisurely than usual, while his room was thoroughly searched. Nothing really suspect was discovered; though a few sketches of the ground-plans of cathedrals in which he had traced the transition from the Romanic form to the Gothic were seized as extremely suspicious. But actually no one took the affair very seriously. Even I, who was ready to credit the Nazis with the most monstrous barbarity, told myself: "It's really very decent of the Government to pro-

tect its adversary from the Brown Horde in this way—for
now, of course, they'll treat themselves to a 'Night of the
Long Knives.'"   One heard that innumerable arrests had
been made, and of all sorts of people: well-known and
unimportant, political and unpolitical. This was reassuring; and so was the term "protective arrest."

But we soon had further news. Many of the prisoners
had been dragged into the SA barracks and horribly maltreated there. Already one began to hear of deaths re-
sulting from ill-treatment. We felt that my son had
been fortunate. He was one of the first to be arrested by
the police and taken to the police-station. Subsequent
arrests were usually effected by the SA and SS, and most
of those who fell into their hands were terribly beaten.

On the following day my son was sent to the Spandau
prison, with a whole batch of doctors, jurists, journalists,
and the like. From Spandau, too, we had reassuring
news. It is true that many of the prisoners found the
primitive conditions intolerable, but they did not trouble
my son, who was used to a Spartan life. Moreover, we
still imagined that we were living in a legal State. When
the "seizure of power" was over, and everything was orderly again, they would, of course, be released, and allowed to go about their business!

My son's worst anxiety was in respect of his office. His
affairs had come to a standstill, for the advocate (Bar-
basch) with whom my son shared his chambers was also
a prisoner in Spandau. My son's young secretary, Mar-

got Fürst, had given birth to her second child only a week earlier. But this did not prevent her from doing her very utmost to deal with the work of the office. An attempt was made to obtain representatives who could at least attend to the most urgent cases. But this was a difficult matter. Many of those who were approached were afraid —and were soundly berated by the plucky little secretary. One of them with whom she was especially angry, because "God knows, they had nothing against him," was beaten to death by the SA a few days later. He had been guilty of giving truthful evidence as eyewitness in a SA murder trial.

And now there began a mass exodus of those advocates who were in the true sense gentlemen of the law, and who had not "regularized" themselves in time. Not one of them dared to show up at his chambers or sign a document. But Margot Fürst had permission to correspond with her employer in Spandau, and in respect of urgent affairs she was even allowed to consult him, in person or over the telephone. And he warned her repeatedly that she must make a note of all losses sustained, in order to provide material for an eventual claim for damages.

We asked Arlsberg[1] to defend Hans. He refused— wisely, in anticipation of what was to come. But he named several advocates, men who were "not in danger," to whom Hans could safely entrust his defence. They

---

[1] Prof. Dr. Max Arlsberg, one of the most reputable lawyers in Berlin. During the first year of Hitler's régime, he committed suicide in Switzerland.

made application to the competent officials, only to be told that for the time being no legal steps could be taken. A few respectable officials (for it had not been possible to make an immediate clearance of all the "unreliable" elements) advised them not to run into danger by acting on Litten's behalf. Some even counselled them to vanish as quickly as possible. And the men so warned were actually arrested in their homes by the stormtroopers.

I did not attempt to obtain a permit to visit my son; I did not even write to him. The letters and visits of his secretary were more important. She understood my son's position better than I, and she was a plucky and indefatigable young woman. I merely provided her with the means of buying all that Hans needed.

In the first week of April Hans wrote from a new address: the Sonnenburg concentration camp! In a short postcard he told us that he was well, that he had merely been moved from one prison to another, and that otherwise nothing was changed. His next letter contained no further news, but we guessed that he must be feeling more despondent, for he mentioned his will, and asked his friend Fürst to sell his valuable library, as he had no further use for it.

At the same time there were rumours flying about the town to the effect that the prisoners under "protective arrest" at Sonnenburg were being hideously maltreated. There was as yet no mention of Hans. But as a measure of precaution I went to the Reichswehr Minister, Herr von Blomberg, and begged him, on the grounds of our old friendly relations, to do what he could for Hans. And I told him of the rumours. If a man in his position were only to telephone to Sonnenburg in order to inquire into the welfare of Hans Litten, a prisoner in "protective custody," this would surely make such an impression on the guards that they would not dare to ill-treat him. He was pleasant and courteous as ever (as General in command in Königsberg he had been a frequent visitor in our house). Of course, if it would make me any easier he would ring up the camp. And on the next opportunity he would speak to Göring. But he laughed at my fears. That anything of the kind of which I dreaded should come to pass was quite out of the question; and even if it should ever happen that such things were done, they would certainly never be done to a man of Litten's reputation. He might be a defeated adversary, who must, of course, be put out of action by means of internment, but everyone had the greatest respect for him, and he would certainly be well treated, if only because of the bad impression it would make on the public if anything were to happen to such a man.

On the following day the rumours were more definite. The *Sonnenburger Zeitung* reported that a convoy of prisoners under "protective arrest" had been marched from the railway station to the Sonnenburg camp singing the Horst Wessel song. The guards had zealously stimulated the singers with their rubber truncheons.

Frau Mühsam told Margot Fürst the following: She had obtained a visitor's permit from the Gestapo on the occasion of her husband's birthday, but on the day before the anniversary she was informed by telegram that he would not find her visit convenient at the moment. A prearranged sign told her that the telegram was not spontaneous, and that it was of the utmost importance that she should not postpone her visit. She succeeded in seeing him for a moment in the courtyard, for she had the Gestapo's permit in her hand. Her husband bore the unmistakable marks of grievous ill-treatment; Caspar, too, could hardly drag himself along. Someone told her in a whisper that Litten was in such a serious condition that even the prisoners were not allowed a glimpse of him.

Frau Mühsam then interviewed some of the townsfolk. She learned that when the prisoners were marched through Sonnenburg the guards had driven them along with kicks and blows of their rubber truncheons. They had also commanded them to sing the Horst Wessel song. As some of the prisoners did not join in the song (and it may be imagined that in those days most people would have refused with disgust to sing "the pimp song," as it was popularly called, so that the demand was an abominable insult), the stormtroopers fell upon the convoy and beat the prisoners so brutally that many of them fell to the ground. The SA men then trampled on them with their nailed boots until they could hardly crawl. Caspar,[1] Litten, Mühsam[2] and Ossietzky[3] were treated the worst.

At the same time a letter arrived from Hans, and from this, now that our eyes had been opened, we could plainly see what had happened. He spoke of the affairs of various imaginary clients, and this is roughly what he said: "What with my own troubles I have quite forgotten certain very important cases. You absolutely must see that they receive careful attention. Baer (his friends used to call him "Bear") positively must be allowed to cancel his leave. He is on such bad terms with the other tenants that they constantly attack him when he comes home at night. They have repeatedly thrashed him with a violence that might very well be fatal. Since all attempts to obtain redress have been unavailing one must try to find another house for him.—And then I am greatly concerned about the Hali case (Ha-ns Li-tten). In his unfortunate situation the man has already made several attempts at suicide. His father, of course, has influential connections, and through them he can surely obtain some reasonable employment for him. It is true that he is on very bad terms with his son, but you must make it clear to him that his life is at stake."

[1] Caspar: President of the Communist group of the Landtag.

[2] Mühsam: Theorist of anarchism, who took part in the Munich "Räterepublic" of 1919. Was arrested on the night of the Reichstag fire and finally murdered in Oranienburg, July, 1934.

[3] Ossietzky: Winner of Nobel Peace Prize and a pacifist. Was arrested on the night of the fire and ill-treated in many camps. He contracted severe tuberculosis and was released in 1937. He died of the disease in the spring of 1938.

That very day I wrote to Blomberg, saying that my fears were unhappily justified; and indeed the actual facts were far more dreadful than anything that I had feared. I begged him most earnestly to keep his promise and take urgent measures to help my son.

With Margot I went to the Gestapo, in order to see the Public Prosecutor, who was in control of the camps in the Berlin district, and who had come into professional contact with Hans and Margot. Outside his door some thirty relatives of prisoners had assembled in order to protest against what was happening at Sonnenburg. Just as I arrived Dr. S. came out of his room and declared that he would see nobody, and that everything was in order at the camp. The others allowed themselves to be dismissed, but Margot and I were obstinate.

After I had made an urgent complaint concerning what had happened, Dr. S. exclaimed: "Things are not really so bad; your son has been knocked about a bit, but actually it was by his fellow-prisoners."

"My son," I replied, "was always greatly beloved. Such a thing would be impossible unless the prisoners had been ordered by the guards to maltreat him."

Dr. S.: "No, no, there's a very simple psychological explanation. Those people see now what they've brought upon themselves, and they are venting their wrath on those who have influenced them and landed them in such a situation."

"I have no right," I said, "to cast doubt on your assertion, but I know one thing for an absolute certainty—that the guards do not merely 'knock people about a bit'; they maltreated them abominably." And I told him in detail what I had heard.

To this Dr. S. replied: "Well, since you have such exact information I will admit that things have happened of which we ourselves disapprove most completely. But we have taken immediate steps to remedy the situation. The SA men have been dismissed and replaced by police. Your son has been placed in solitary confinement, so that he is protected from any further attacks. You can be completely reassured."

And I was actually reassured, and even now I am convinced that Dr. S., who gave me the impression that he was a thoroughly decent human being, was himself convinced of the complete success of the steps which he had taken.

But my son's next letter told me that his situation was worse than ever. Once more disguising the facts as the details of fictitious lawsuits, he explained that solitary confinement made it possible for his captors to torture him without fear of being disturbed. He begged us to use all the influence we possessed on his behalf.

I explained to Dr. S. in the most urgent and emphatic terms that the steps which he had taken were quite useless, and that on the contrary the situation was worse than ever. I told him that all Berlin was full of the reports of these atrocities; that one could not enter a café, or an underground railway-train, without hearing of these horrible brutalities. The only disturbing remark which I quoted from my son's letter was his apology for writing so badly, because he had no spectacles.

I asked for a permit to visit him immediately.

Dr. S.: "I can't give you a permit, as your son's secretary has already received permission to visit him."

"That," I replied, "is on account of professional affairs. I, as his mother, have a better right to see him than his secretary."

Dr. S.: "But I have really allowed more visits already than I can justify."

"Nevertheless, I as his mother have a right to see him. I have waited long enough."

Dr. S.: "Later; for technical reasons a visit isn't possible now."

"For me, this refusal is proof that my son is in such a condition that you can't let him be seen. I hold you responsible for my son's life."

Dr. S.: "But really, I can't always be present and see that nothing happens to your son!"

"You have control over the camp," I replied. "You could give orders that the brutalities are to stop. I suppose, after all, you are in a position to see that order is kept in the camp?"

Dr. S.: "The trouble is that your son is so hated by the SA that with the best will in the world one can't protect him."

"If I were in your position," I said, "I could protect him."

Dr. S.: "What would you do?"

"I should go there immediately," I said, "and let him tell you in a private interview what has happened; and I should make a physical examination. Then, if you were once convinced of the brutalities which you now don't believe were serious, you would see to it that the SA behaved themselves properly. For my part, I should never expect that criminals would behave decently merely because they were dressed up in the clothes of decent men. You have not withdrawn the murder squad 33 (this was the company which my son had proved guilty of a whole series of murders) ; you have simply mixed them with the police and put them into police uniforms!"

He actually promised me that on the following day, when he had some sort of business at the camp, he would look into my son's case. I told him that I was pulling all the strings I could on behalf of my son, and that I should ask my friend the Reichswehr Minister von Blomberg to help me.

The following night I spent in a railway-carriage, for I had really made up my mind to "pull all the strings I could." Hans had already been a month at Sonnenburg. I went to see Prince Wilhelm of Prussia, with whom my husband was on terms of friendship. He was not in the least surprised by my request, for he knew very well what was happening. "But," he said, "I have no influence whatever, and I can't run any risks, for I'm in danger as a Stahlhelmer. I must be thankful if the fellows leave me in peace."

"Could you," I said, "give me a recommendation to your relative, August Wilhelm? He will have some influence; he has been a Nazi for a long while; perhaps he will help me?"

Prince Wilhelm laughed. "Auwi? No, our whole family broke off all connection with him officially when he became a Nazi."

"And the Crown Prince?"

"Yes, he of course would be willing to help you, but will he have any influence? Besides, he's in Italy; he's always changing his address; you can reach him only through the Embassy. And a difficult business like this can hardly be settled by letter. But what about Prince F.? He, after all, is an intimate friend of August Wilhelm's."

But Prince F. was no more helpful. "Prince Auwi? Impossible; we have nothing to do with him since he joined the party. We have even had violent quarrels in the Press. Besides, my own position is shaky. I'm afraid I myself may be given the boot any day."

We went over the list of all our common acquaintances. The decent ones were all without influence, and most of them were actually in danger. From the others, who had quickly joined the big battalions at the last moment, no help could be expected. Prince Wilhelm gave me an introduction to a leading Stahlhelmer in Berlin, on whom I called a few days later. "I myself," he explained, "am at the present moment in a dangerous situation, owing to my intimacy with Düsterberg, whom they have just thrown out. I am trying night and day to get Stahlhelmer out of the torture-chambers of the SA, but I seldom have any success. I will try to interest a few safer people in your son's case."

While Prince F. and I were racking our brains to discover whether there was not, in our large circle of acquaintances, a single human who was both unimperilled and influential, my second son, Heinz, rang me up from Berlin. Dr. S. had just called him up to say that I could visit my son in Spandau. It transpired that Dr. S. had been to Sonnenburg and had been so shocked by Hans' condition that to save him he had at once transferred Hans by car to Spandau.

CHAPTER III

Spandau—Not Yet "Regularized"

I RETURNED HOME by the night train, and after learning what there was to learn I went at once to the Gestapo. There, again, outside Dr. S.'s door, was an endless queue of people waiting to see him. When I had waited for half an hour I looked so ill, after two nights in the train, that someone advised me to sit down and rest on a bench which stood at some little distance. I objected that I should lose my turn, and since there was such a crowd I should probably never see Dr. S. at all. At this there was a positive outburst of indignation. What was I thinking? Of course they would keep my place for me!—The people who were waiting here were all relatives of prisoners under "protective arrest"; that is, they were respectable people.

While I was sitting on the bench an SA man passed me who was just the sort of type I could imagine as one of the Sonnenburg guard. I suppose my expression, as I watched him, must have reflected my feelings very eloquently, for a man in civilian dress (I think he was a clerk in the Gestapo) whispered to me: "When one's eyes are so full of hatred it's better to shut them."

I understood then why Heinz had always dragged me round a corner so quickly, or into a shop, when we met SA troops marching through the streets. He had always told me that my face wore an expression of such passionate hatred and contempt that it might easily get me into trouble. And this was long before I had any personal experience of the SA. My hatred was really due to an incident which did not concern me personally.

A few months before the *coup d'état* I was cheerfully returning home, with a number of acquaintances, from a theatrical performance in Chemnitz. Suddenly we found ourselves in the midst of a large troop of SA men, who were going home from a meeting. They were going in our direction, and it seemed impossible to escape from the press. I told my friends: "I've got to get out of this; I can't stand it among these fellows, they smell of blood." The response to this was a chorus of loud yells and laughter from the SA. My friends, who were not used to such behaviour on my part, and were thoroughly alarmed by my incautiousness and my pallor, silenced me, and forced a way for me out of the crowd.

Next morning we read in the newspaper: "A troop of SA men, returning from a Party meeting, gave chase to an apprentice who belonged to the SAJ (the Socialist Labour Youth). The youth finally succeeded in escaping into a house through an open door, but the SA men followed him in and beat him to death." Since that day I was always conscious of the same smell of blood when

I saw a troop of SA men, and I thought with anxiety of my son, whom they hated, and whom they had already attacked, in empty streets, in a station of the Underground, and even in a little café. . . .

At last it was my turn. "You can visit your son," Dr. S. told me; "I took him in my own car to Spandau." I thanked him; and then he asked me: "Have you yet written to the Prime Minister Göring?" No, I had not. "Then who has written to him?"

"You will remember," I replied, "that when I last came to see you I told you that I should make all possible use of my connections, and that I should begin by writing to Herr von Blomberg. I think it is not impossible that he may have written to the Prime Minister."

"Well," said Dr. S., "I had already taken your son to Spandau before I received these instructions."

Whatever these "instructions," Dr. S. was replaced a few weeks later by a much stricter official, with whom none of the prisoners' relatives could obtain an interview. The general opinion was that Dr. S. had lost his position on account of his intervention in the case of my son.

I drove straight to Spandau, and before long I stood face to face with my son. He came up to me with a radiant smile, saying that I had been wonderful (and it was only from Dr. S. that he could have heard what I had been doing), and that at the moment he was so comfortable that he really couldn't wish for anything better. He added: "Dr. S. has saved my life." Even the guard wore a beaming smile.   It was really a happy interview.

At the same time, he looked very strange; his face was swollen; the shape of his head was altogether peculiar; it seemed lower and broader, and somehow unsymmetrical. He told me that he was suffering from violent pains in the head, and that the doctor had warned him that it was difficult to treat them properly, as in order to do the pains any good he ought to be a great deal in the open air, but the state of his leg made it necessary, for the present, to lie down.

From our conversation during subsequent visits, from cautious inquiries of the prison warders, and from a talk with the prison doctor, I discovered that there were serious injuries to the leg, the jawbone had been fractured, and a number of teeth had been broken off short.   At the same time there were injuries to the middle ear and one eye (the sight of which was never fully restored). The pains in the head, which never quite disappeared, were caused, according to the doctor, by a periostitis. Probably, too, there was a fracture of the cheekbone under the injured eye.   This could not be determined without an X-ray photograph, which could not be taken in the camp.   However, the doctor assured me that this diagnosis was not essential; it would not lead to any change in the treatment of the case.

My son was in such a state of health that he would be kept in solitary confinement as long as he was at Spandau;

but his own assurances, and the whole atmosphere of the place, convinced me that everything that could be done to cure him was being done, and that all the warders were treating him as well as they could without losing their jobs. One had only to look at their faces to see that they had a sort of affection for him.

Sometimes the visitors had to wait for hours before their names were called. As far as I can remember, one visit a month was allowed, and then one could talk with the prisoner for twenty minutes. Margot often received a permit between the official dates, as she had to consult him in respect of the affairs of his clients. On the occasion of one such visit Hans gave her a scrap of paper on which a primitive code was written: the first letter of the fourth word of each sentence would convey a message.

The warder declared that he had seen my son give Margot a note, but he was quite satisfied when she quietly offered him her handbag, saying: "Please look through my bag and see if you can find anything. How can you think we should be so foolish?"

The next letter from Hans contained a message in this code, asking for poison. (For safety, because he had so longed for it in Sonnenburg.) He gave exact instructions as to the kind of poison, and the quantity: it was to be packed in a nib-box and concealed in a pat of butter. No doctor would give us a prescription for such a poison; but we obtained it at last from a friend of my son's who was employed in a chemist's shop.

Despite the amiability of the warders, the length of our interview was restricted to twenty minutes, as there were always other visitors waiting. The dates of all visits were arranged in accordance with the alphabetical order of the prisoners' names. The prisoners' relatives had simply to send in their names to the inspector; having received a permit, they had to wait in the waiting-room, which was always full of women, until their turn came. I never saw a male visitor there.

Many of these simple-minded women had saved a little money to give to their husbands. It was always confiscated immediately, "in order to cover the cost of the prisoners' maintenance"; so one of the women warned the occupants of the waiting-room never to bring any money. I myself should not have done so in any case, for during my first visit Hans had told me: "I don't want any extra grub. Never send me anything I haven't asked for." If I remember rightly, a parcel of soiled linen was to be called for every week, and a parcel containing clean linen and food was to be left. (The clothing fetched away from Sonnenburg had bloodstains upon it.) These parcels were always taken to the camp by Margot or myself, as by this means we were able to keep in touch with the staff. We sent Hans sweetmeats, fruit, and vegetables. Thanks to his simple tastes, he was quite content with the prisoners' diet; except that it troubled him greatly—since he was a strict vegetarian—that he could not remove every trace of meat from the stew. But he soon realized that this diet was not sufficient without the herring or the slice of sausage which was given to the prisoners at supper; so he decided to accustom himself to "eating corpses."

Among the many visitors there was one woman whose case I thought particularly moving. She was always sitting in the waiting-room on my arrival, accompanied by a basket which contained quite a respectable menu. It was taken as a matter of course that all those visitors who had not to catch a train should give her precedence, lest the food should grow cold. Her husband, she told us, couldn't get on with the food at all; it was simply uneatable; so before every visit she prepared his favourite dishes, and it delighted her to see how he enjoyed them; for they actually allowed him to eat them during her visit. I wondered why she was so anxious to see him eat, for there cannot have been much time left for conversation. "Oh, well," she explained, "there's not much that one can say; it's enough for me to see how he enjoys his food."

I, on the contrary, found that there was a great deal that one could say; and one did not need to be so terribly cautious, for the warders here were human beings. Of course, we could not discuss what had happened at Sonnenburg, or talk politics. But I was able to tell Hans that I had been to see von Blomberg, Prince Wilhelm, and others; that to my thinking he was for the time being better off and safer in camp than he would have been at liberty; and that my influential friends had expressed the opinion that we had better not attempt to effect any change for the present. The prisoners all seemed to know of the brutalities and murders which were being committed in the outer world, and Hans apparently agreed with me. "But," he objected, "this state of affairs may very well continue for another five years."

I answered indignantly: "Don't talk such nonsense; it won't last six months!" and the warder growled consolingly: "Not so long; there can be all sorts of changes in six months."

When my son's birthday came round I took him his favourite dishes, and obtained permission for their delivery from the office. They had already filled out a visitor's permit for me, and when I called attention to the fact that my visit was not yet due, I was told: "Yes, we know that. But do you really think we could send you away on your son's thirtieth birthday without having seen him?" And one of the officials added, regretfully: "Such a genius, and laid on the shelf at the age of thirty!"

Instead of examining the books which I had brought with me, page by page, as the regulations required, the competent official quickly turned over the leaves. We began to talk about my son, and it appeared from what was said that the greatest care was being taken of his health. It was true that he had been given a cell to himself, but this was on account of the state of his health; and as it was not good for him to be alone all day, since his nerves were still badly affected, he was given a companion during the daytime: a man with whom he got on excellently. They were working together on the comparative history of the artistic and cultural evolution of different historical periods. It amused the officials to see how absorbed they were in their work, and it helped my son to forget his pains.

I saw this companion of my son's shortly after his discharge. Since he still felt that he was closely watched, we met in the house of a friend of mine. He had much to tell me of his stimulating intercourse with Hans, and of the universal esteem in which he was held by the other prisoners. They were amazed to discover that he knew Sanskrit and Hebrew as well as the more usual languages, and could read Chinese and Arabic authors in the original. His good memory enabled him to manage with a comparatively small number of books. One day, when Goethe was discussed, he quoted so extensively from a comparatively unfamiliar work of Goethe's that they took it for granted that he had just been reading it, until they had convinced themselves that there was no copy of the book in Spandau. With Father Stratmann, another internee, he often had the most impassioned discussions on religious subjects. I heard it said more than once: "If they had been longer together Hans would have gone over to Rome." And later on I was constantly hearing of my son's leanings toward Catholicism. But he could no more have joined a rigid religious community than he could bring himself to submit to the ties of a political party. He was in everything an independent. A colleague once asked him, when on getting to know him better he was astonished to find how completely they agreed in respect of their political views: "Shall we two found a party?" But Hans only laughed, and replied: "Two are too many for my party."

I asked this fellow-prisoner of Hans to tell me what had happened at Sonnenburg; for I was sure that my son must have told him. At first he absolutely refused to speak of the affair. Hans had so often exclaimed: "My mother must never know what was done to me." I managed with some difficulty to convince him that I could tackle the Gestapo much more effectually if I could appeal to the facts. He told me then what had long been generally known: he described the brutal beating of the prisoners, the trampling with nailed boots, and the mock executions, when the victims were stood against a wall, expecting to be shot. But the execution was "postponed," or the Nazis would fire wide of the mark, saying: "We're just having a little practice. To-morrow you'll be shot in earnest."

At last he escaped further torment by making a deposition, but after this he refused to speak further. What the Nazis wanted was incriminating material to enable them to hunt down the men acquitted in the Felseneck case. Some SA men entered my son's cell at night, saying: "Now you are going to be shot. But we want a souvenir of your fear of death. You'll be photographed as the shots are fired." A revolver was pressed against each temple. The flashlight was ignited; the shutter clicked; but no shots were fired. With such "jests" as this, and others of the kind, the SA men amused themselves for hours, and even for days.

CHAPTER IV

The Gestapo Interrogates

THE GENERAL ATMOSPHERE of Spandau had so far reassured me that I ventured on a holiday away from home. But a letter from Hans made me break off my journey. It contained, in code, the information that Dr. S. had been replaced by Dr. Conrady, who was famed for his severity, and that the outlook was bad. I decided that I must be on the spot if there were going to be changes for the worse.

On my next visit to Spandau (in the middle of August) I was told that my son was just being taken away, but I could speak to him for a moment in the inspector's office. Even before the door was opened I could hear his excited voice: "Then haven't you forwarded my letter to the Gestapo?" And when the inspector replied, reassuringly, that he had done so, and that there was no cause for uneasiness, Hans exclaimed: "But there is; I am being taken away by the very man who has threatened to have me manhandled."

I was able to talk to Hans only for a few minutes. I could feel how violently his heart was beating. His hands were cold as ice. When I realized that he was going to be cross-examined, I told him: "You must tell them all they want to know. The new government has established new ideas of morality; you have to submit to them, even if you don't share them. If you do anything immoral the government is responsible, not you!"

He replied: "It isn't only a question of violating my professional secrecy; I am required to testify to things that are not true!"

"You definitely can't help the man," I said: "they'll do what they like with him, whether you stick to the truth or not. Tell them what they want!" With that our interview ended; my son was taken away in the prison van.

The inspector reproached me for losing my head: whether because I had given my son immoral advice, or because I had put him in the unpleasant situation of overhearing my speech and reporting it, since it was possible that the constables waiting outside had heard me, I cannot say.

I hurried to the nearest telephone and tried to ring up Herr von Blomberg. He was out of town, and his personal adjutant was with him, so that nothing could be done in that direction.

I drove to the address of a woman of my acquaintance, a National Socialist, who was staying in Berlin for the time being, and of whose decency of character I had evidence. We took counsel together, and agreed to go first of all to a friend of Blomberg's with whom we had once been on the very best of terms. He explained that he himself, as a Stahlhelmer, was not *persona grata*, and that no one took the slightest notice of him; which, in view of his opinions, was the best thing that could happen. And, of course, he was quite without influence.

Then the three of us went into consultation. He suggested the army chaplain Müller, who was then in Berlin, as he was about to be enthroned as *Reichsbischof*. Müller had once courted the lovely young woman who was so anxious to help me, and after he had christened her firstborn he had kissed her in anything but a parsonical manner. He was known to pride himself on his success with the fair sex; in short, I hoped that my friend would be able to talk him into adopting a helpful attitude. The good-natured officer allowed her to use his telephone, though the conversation that followed might have been disastrous to both of them.

She could not get Müller, who was then attending a conference, but she did at least get his right hand, Meusel (who shot himself later on, having discovered that the *Reichsbischof* was his wife's lover). She told Meusel that the most scandalous things were happening; it was he who converted her to National Socialism, and unless she was to feel ashamed of her conversion something must be done to stop them.

She succeeded, at last, in making arrangements for a midnight supper with the *Reichsbischof*. Unfortunately nothing came of it. After she had told him what was amiss, he exclaimed: "Do you really believe that as my very first action in my capacity of Reichsbischof I could help a Communist?" And in the course of their further conversation the Christian gentleman added: "The Communists have got to be exterminated, root and stem."

Next morning all the newspapers contained the same report, under headlines which were printed in extra large type: "Hans Litten Confesses: Accessory to Murder." Under this was the statement that Hans Litten had confessed that he had defended a man who had shot down an SA man in the Felseneck affair, although he knew that his client was guilty. This statement was followed by the most ferocious abuse of the advocate who had defended a confessed murderer, etc.

I was quite satisfied with this, for now, I thought, the matter was settled and done with. But on the following day we received a terribly excited letter from Hans, from which we drew the conclusion that he intended to take his life. He was also greatly perturbed at having heard nothing more from me. Probably he thought I had been arrested after my last conversation with him. Margot immediately went to Spandau. She would see him if possible, and try to calm him. We hoped that she would be admitted, as she was on good terms with the inspector. I was afraid, on the other hand, that he would not admit me, because he was so annoyed with me on account of my last interview.

But when she reached the camp the ambulance had just taken my son to Moabit. She was shown into the inspector's room, and there, from the excited mood of the officials, and from various conversations over the telephone, she probably gathered more than she would have been told under ordinary circumstances. And this is what she learned:

Hans had returned one day from his cross-examination in a state of complete distraction. He had immediately written a report to the Gestapo that he had given his evidence under compulsion, that his deposition was not in accordance with the truth, and that he now repudiated it. Since he dreaded the consequences of this repudiation, he was about to take his life. As he was in solitary confinement he was able to make the necessary preparations unobserved.

He was found next morning unconscious and bloodless; it was thought at first that he was dead. But the doctor who was summoned—a fellow-prisoner—succeeded in calling him back to life. He had taken the poison which had been smuggled into the camp in a pat of butter, and when he began to bring it up he cut the arteries of his wrists in four places with a razor-blade. That he did not bleed to death was explained by the fact that the arteries had contracted, and the blood had to some extent coagulated over the wounds.

Hans had written a farewell letter to me. This the Gestapo must have forwarded to the censor; I never received it. He had also written a farewell letter to the inspector, in which he apologized for causing him such inconvenience. He was afraid that he would be upsetting the inspector's arrangements for going on leave in two days' time, and he would willingly have postponed his suicide; but it was impossible to delay his repudiation of his evidence for so long. He assured the inspector that he had had the poison which he had taken on his person at the time of his arrest, but it had not been discovered when he was searched. He said this to protect the officials from any unpleasant consequences. But he had, without suspecting it, subjected them to much more serious unpleasantness. They had been ordered to put Hans in irons every night, but no one had obeyed this order; they were unwilling to torture their prisoner.

Directly I heard that Hans had attempted suicide I rang up the Moabit Infirmary. Schlegel, the director, told me that I could see my son, but I must obtain a permit from the Gestapo. I must not lose a moment, for in all probability Hans had not long to live.

At the office of the Gestapo they seemed to have had word of my coming. They took me and Margot, who had accompanied me, straight to the Criminal Commissioner Marowski, who had conducted the cross-examination. "Of course," he said, "you can see him immediately. I'll take you there in my car to save time." I do not think he was prompted to make this offer by a guilty conscience, or by humanitarian motives; it was simply that he wanted, during the journey, to question me unobtrusively.

He began by asking me whether I had obtained the poison for my son. I was greatly astonished that anyone should imagine that a mother would buy poison in order to enable her son to commit suicide.

Then he asked me: "Do you think your son tried to kill himself because he felt that his honour was called in question by the newspaper reports?"

"That," I said, "is quite out of the question. I am sure that my son would think as I do—namely, that only he himself could destroy his honour."

"That," said Marowski, "sets my mind at rest. I was reproaching myself for allowing the Press to get hold of the report."

He continued: "I have been on bad terms with your son for a long while now; we used to be at daggers drawn over all sorts of questions. But that's of no consequence whatever; that didn't influence me in any way.... Now, what do you know of this business?"

"I know absolutely nothing," I replied.

"But you must know something," he objected. "You told him: 'After all, you can't do anything to help the man!' You couldn't have made such a remark if you had known nothing."

"No," I persisted, "I know absolutely nothing whatever. What I said to my son is explained by my attitude to you. I took it for granted that if you cross-examined my son it must be because you wanted to learn something that he would not willingly tell you. It's only natural that I should say 'the man,' because it wouldn't have occurred to me that a woman might be in question. And if I immediately thought of the Felseneck affair in connection with such a cross-examination, that again is perfectly natural, for that was the trial which had recently caused so much bad feeling."

"But," he said, "you must surely have been in your son's confidence. It would, after all, be only natural that he should have told you all about the Felseneck trial." And when I answered in the negative, he exclaimed: "But you really can't ask me to believe that you never discussed such matters!"

Then I explained that my son and I lived in different parts of the country—my son in Berlin, and I in Königsberg; also, that he was on bad terms with my husband, on account of political differences, so that we had met only when I had been passing through Berlin.

"Well, do you tell me that in Berlin you never discussed such matters?"

"Never. In the first place, I think all politics are hateful; and secondly, I have seen how differences of political opinion are poisoning family life, especially since the National Socialists have been so powerful. There were finer and pleasanter things to talk about in the little time we had together."

Herr Marowski was just on the point of making me

clearly understand what a shocking individual my son must be, since he had always been kind and friendly to the most horrible criminals, and that it was really most extraordinary that a man of such good family should behave in such a way, when we reached the infirmary, and our dialogue was interrupted.

The director, Sanitatsrät Schlegel, was waiting for me. "Don't be startled," he said. "Your son looks terrible."

"Will you be able to save his life?" I asked.

He replied, emphatically: "You may be sure that I shall do all that is in my power. I must naturally save him for the State; the State wants further evidence from him."

"If that is so," I said, "I would rather my son had not been brought back to life."

"When we have his evidence," Schlegel replied, "he can do what he likes to himself. We take no further interest in him after that."

My son looked like a corpse. He was not yet fully conscious, and at first he did not recognize Margot and myself. They had applied the stomach-pump, sewn up the gashes in his wrists, and given him intravenous injections to replace the lost blood. When he slowly recovered consciousness the Commissar, who with his assistant had accompanied us to the bedside, asked my son: "Do you feel strong enough yet to answer a few questions?"

One could see that Hans was making a convulsive effort to collect his faculties. "I'll try," he answered. I wanted to protest, but then I reflected that it might comfort Hans if I were present at the cross-examination. And I hoped to learn something of what had been happening hitherto.

"Why," Marowski asked, "did you attempt to commit suicide?"

"Because all the evidence I gave was false. I had to repudiate it; but I didn't feel that I could bear the consequences with which I was threatened in the case of such repudiation. I wrote to the Gestapo and told them so."

Marowski was visibly alarmed. "Did you mention my name in your letter?"

"Yes," Hans replied.

"But you gave me your word," cried Marowski angrily, "that you would make no use of anything that passed at a private interview."

"I only mentioned what you dictated to the secretary."

The male nurse, seeing that Hans was losing consciousness again, felt his pulse. "The conversation must be discontinued," he said. Marowski left the room with the words: "I shall have more questions to ask in a few days." To this my son replied in a distressed whisper: "No, please ask them here."

On one of my later visits to the infirmary I asked him the meaning of the words "ask them here." He explained: "Here in the infirmary if they torture me during the cross-examination a nurse comes if I cry out, in order to stop the examination, but in the Gestapo I am absolutely in their power." And he said, on another occasion: "It would have been all right if they had shot me, but I can't bear this badgering and torturing any longer." I could never induce him to speak more definitely of what had happened when he was questioned by the Gestapo.

When I was asked to leave the infirmary I went straight back to the Gestapo. The new Public Prosecutor, Dr. Conrady, who now had charge of the administration of the camps, received me in his office. He was a tall man, good-looking according to Nazi standards of beauty, but his eyes were hard and cold; they seemed to turn green when he lost his temper. Apparently he wanted to intimidate me; he treated me to a penetrating stare as I sat in front of his desk, much as the detective glares at his victim in a crude detective romance. I stared back at him, to show that I was not to be intimidated by such buffoonery. Margot was sitting a little to one side of me. The situation was becoming ridiculous, as neither of us was willing to beat a retreat.

At last he spoke. "Well, what do you want?"

I explained that I was bound to protest against the whole affair: whereupon he declared that he had not the least idea what I was talking about.

"It's impossible," I replied, "that you, in your position, don't know what I have come about. You must have read my son's letter to the Gestapo."

"No," said Conrady, "I have not read it."

"But it's out of the question that a letter containing matter of such importance should not come into your hands!"

"Ach," he exclaimed, "you must just consider what a mass of business I have to deal with. I simply haven't come to your son's affair yet."

"Well," I said, "I can hardly imagine that a case of such importance would not have been brought to your attention before anything else." (Conrady, of course, was perfectly familiar with the details of the case, or he would not have received me. He simply wanted to hear what I should say about it.)

"Well," he said, "tell me now what you are talking about."

I told him briefly how the matter stood. "To begin with," I said, "I protest against the conduct of the cross-examination by the Criminal Commissioner Marowski. He was on very bad terms with my son (I had learned this from Margot), as he himself has told me. And I know that some time ago my son published an article complaining of his improper methods of interrogating defendants. It is perfectly obvious that this man, who behaved so brutally even before the coup d'état,[1] is now venting his wrath upon my son."

"You can't protest against that," said Conrady.

"But one has the right to refuse to be tried before a judge whom one believes to be prejudiced."

---

[1] *Machtergreifung* = seizure of power.

"Before a judge—that'a a different matter. You can't do anything against a Criminal Commissioner."

"Secondly," I continued, "I protest absolutely against this kind of cross-examination."

Conrady merely smiled; he did not think such a ridiculous protest worthy of a rejoinder. "Your son," he declared, "will be cross-examined further until we get the truth out of him."

"You know the truth now," I said.

"No," he retorted, "I am convinced that his first statements were true. The repudiation is false."

"How dare you say that!" I cried. "If my son's deposition had been in accordance with the truth he would have had absolutely no reason for repudiating it and taking his life."

As Conrady continued to insist on his conviction that the first deposition was true, I replied: "My son is a religious man. It is highly improbable that he would leave the world with a lie, for which he would have to answer before God. No man who believes in God could accept such a supposition."

"You seem to assume that I don't believe in God," said Conrady, cynically. "But I do."

At this I could not refrain from saying: "Then I am greatly astonished at your behaviour. And I can only tell you this—I look forward to the moment when we shall stand face to face at the last judgment. Then our rôles will be reversed—if there is a God."

"Well," said Conrady, "I don't in the least believe that your son's attempt at suicide was seriously intended. He is simply play-acting."

"That," I said, "is merely ridiculous. Do you really believe that anyone could time such a thing so exactly? They thought he was dead when they found him."

"Well," said Conrady, "he wouldn't have worried if it had come to that. He was quite ready to die if he could cause us any unpleasantness. I know the man; I was present at the Felseneck trials." His eyes were green with hatred.

I asked him to see that the report in the Press was corrected—and that the news of my son's repudiation of his evidence and his attempted suicide was published. His reply to this demand was an outburst of hilarity.

I continued to reproach him for the methods employed in cross-examination, and at last he exclaimed: "But all these assumptions of yours are nonsensical. As far as I am concerned, you can convince yourself by personal observation as to the procedure in such an examination. You can be present at the examination to-morrow."

From my further conversation with Conrady it appeared that he knew of my husband's political activities (he had been a member of the German People's Party, had contributed political articles to the Press, and had taken an active part in the electoral contest); he was informed as to Heinz's artistic views and political opinions; but he did not even know that I had a third son; my youngest boy had not yet made himself obnoxious to Germany's rulers.

"Your husband," he said, reproachfully, "keeps out of the way in Czechoslovakia, and you have just been there yourself."

"You mean," I replied, "in Sudeten Germany!"

"Well, isn't that Czechoslovakia?"

"Don't you know," I replied, "that good Germans regard it as their duty to spend their holidays in the German-speaking *Ausland?* We went to show our *Volksgenossen* that we are all one people. From East Prussia we visit the Memel district; from Berlin we go to the Sudeten Germans."

That silenced him, but his eyes were green again. Evidently the irony of my remarks had not escaped him.

Next morning, when I called on Marowski at the hour appointed, he declared that he had not the slightest intention of allowing me to be present at the examination, even though I had Dr. Conrady's permission. Moreover, the examination would not be held for some days; he had to collect more material.

I did what I could with Conrady. I believed, of course, that any examination which took place in my presence would be the merest farce; I was quite convinced that it would be followed by an examination of a very different kind; but I thought it important to gain some insight into what was happening. Conrady declared that he could not possibly compel Marowski to admit me. His promise had, of course, been conditional upon Marowski's consent.

When I asked if I could not at least visit my son, he replied that there had been no question of a visit; only of my presence at a cross-examination. I tried what amiability would do; I was sure he would never be so cruel as to forbid me to see my son when he was struggling back to life.

"No," said Conrady, "I am not a monster. As far as I am concerned you can see him again to-day. But I must warn you that in accordance with the regulations you can't see him again for three months."

"I thought," I said, "that in your high position you could make such regulations yourself."

He was rather flattered at this. "I can, of course, but for that very reason I mustn't take advantage of my position."

"But I must see my son this day week!" I said.

"That's quite out of the question."

"Have you really the heart," I said, "to forbid me to visit my son on my birthday?"

He looked at me doubtfully.

"You think I'm lying!" I cried. "Well, when I call for the permit I'll bring my birth certificate!"

"Well, you can see him again in a week, but that's definitely the last time."

A week later, when I called again, I silently handed

him my birth certificate. "That wasn't really necessary," he said, in some embarrassment. And after a pause: "We are very much annoyed about your son. God knows, he's in an appalling position; he really needn't make things worse for himself."

"In God's name," I cried, "what has he done now?"

"He keeps on telling us a pack of lies. He's lying all the time. We shall soon lose patience with him!"

"You are still going on the preconceived opinion that his confession was genuine. You are deceiving yourselves; my son is telling the truth now!"

"We know," said Conrady, "that your son persists in lying. We have proof of it; we know."

"Evidence," I said, "can be deceptive. Two months ago I read a newspaper report to the effect that the man had at last been discovered who shot the SA man Schwarz in the Felseneck fight. He had confessed to the shooting in the camp. And his name was quite different from the name you are concerned with now. I can't possibly assume that you would have published such a report in all the newspapers if you had not believed that you had conclusive evidence."

"As a laywoman," said Conrady, "you can't form any judgment. Our only interest in the matter is to learn the truth. How would it profit us to get a false confession from him?"

"I have been wondering," I replied. "I assume that you believe that in a certain man, namely, Ackert, you have the murderer, but you can't induce him to confess. And it is, after all, unaesthetic to sentence a man who hasn't confessed to his crime. And you think you can obtain a confession if my son would admit that *he* had obtained a confession from the man when he was his client."

"We want to know the truth," said Conrady, and he added, in a very menacing tone: "And we shall cross-examine your son until we have got the truth out of him."

"Would you allow me," I asked, "to tell my son of our conversation? Perhaps I could learn how the matter really stands."

Conrady replied with emphasis: "Yes, yes, do that!"

I told the male nurse that I had to give my son a message from Dr. Conrady. I was therefore able to talk to him without interruption. I advised him most earnestly simply to say what these people wanted him to say; after all, nothing he could do would save Ackert, and he knew what would be the consequences of his attitude. They would simply torture him again until he had made the required admission.

But Hans objected: "What I say is the truth. My client never confessed to me that he shot Schwarz. I am convinced that he did not shoot him. It's of no use to say anything untrue. You see what came of it the first time, when I allowed myself to be induced by torture to make a false deposition. That won't happen a second time. As far as that goes, it would be a stupid thing to do. If I once begin telling them lies I shall involve myself in contradictions, and then they can easily prove that I've been lying. Besides, it's horrible, the things they want me to say. Do you know Rechtsanwalt Sack?"

"Is that the man who defended Torgler in the Reichstag fire trial?"

"Yes. Just go to him and ask him what he knows about me. I'm involved in that affair too."

Here the orderly interrupted us, saying: "You mustn't talk about that." I promised Hans that I would see Sack at once; and with that my visit was ended.

I rang up Conrady and asked him whether I might tell him what I had learned from my son. For the first time he seemed to welcome the idea of an interview; he replied that I could come at once. Apparently he expected to hear that I had persuaded Hans to make a fresh admission. When I gave him an exact account of our conversation he lost his temper for a moment, and shouted at me.

"How dare you advise your son to tell lies! What sort of a position are you putting me in if you tell him that I sent you and then advise him to lie?"

"But how can you reproach me for that?" I asked. "After all, that is what you wanted me to do!"

"No," he said. "I gain nothing by that. I want the truth, and nothing more. I am extremely surprised that you should do such a thing. After this I can't let you go to see your son again!"

"I admit," I said, "that I behaved wrongly. But for quite another reason. One ought not to advise a man like my son to give such immoral evidence. But during my whole interview with him I had your threat before my eyes in letters of fire: 'We shall lose patience with him!' What that means, in the case of the Gestapo, I can imagine."

He went on scolding me for a while, and then I said that it had certainly been clearly understood that it was my wish that my son should make another false admission. Still, I was willing once more to make it perfectly clear that it had not been his, Conrady's wish. But for that purpose I must, of course, have another permit. However, he would not agree to this, but went on fuming.

I then wrote my son a letter, in which I explained that I had now realized that I had been greatly at fault in advising him to give false evidence, and I begged him to act as his conscience dictated. Then, for weeks, I did not hear from him, although we were allowed to exchange letters weekly as long as he was in the infirmary. When I complained of this to Dr. Conrady I found that our whole correspondence passed through the hands of the Gestapo, and was censored by Conrady himself. During this period my son received no letter from me.

I called on Dr. Sack and told him of my conversation with my son. He declared that there must be a misunderstanding; he had gone through the whole of the documents relating to the Reichstag fire trial, and my son's name was never mentioned, nor was there any allusion to him. I asked him if he would defend my son if any charge should be brought against him. "Of course I would," he said, "but only under the condition that he can prove that he is innocent."

Dr. Sack impressed me as an amiable and complacent gentleman whose practice was prospering enormously, and with whom it was hardly possible to talk, because one's conversation was constantly interrupted by long parleys over the telephone. Apparently his practice had benefited greatly as a result of his defence of Torgler.

When Hans was removed from Spandau his books and manuscripts were confiscated and sent to the Gestapo. I had been horrified to note, on one of my visits, that Hans had destroyed none of our letters. And these letters contained all sorts of news—for example, the way in which the poison was obtained—in the easily decipherable code. This was most unfortunate, for it meant that we could not use the code any longer. It was absolutely necessary that we should give Hans a new code, or nothing of importance could be said in the strictly censored letters.

The new code must be difficult to decipher. But it was necessary to take the conditions of life in the camp into account. A prisoner seldom had much leisure for writing and reading letters; and he was under observation, so that he could not refer to a diagram or a table. We decided to stick to the old code in principle: that is, the first letter of the fourth word of each sentence would serve as a key to the message. But the sequence of the letters of the message was changed beforehand with the help of a key word. As a key word we chose the word *Denkmalsfigur*. The message was ciphered in this way: each letter of the message was replaced by the letter which followed it in the word *Denkmalsfigur*. If the letter did not occur in the key word it was left unchanged. Thus, D became E, E became N, N became K, and so on down to U, which became R. The last letter, R, was replaced by the first, D.

For example, if one wanted to write the word *Gift* (poison), the key word transformed this into *Ugit*. Now the four letters of the word *Ugit* had to form the first letters of the fourth words of the first four sentences of the letter. So the letter might begin as follows: "Gestern waren Walter und Werner bei mir. Walter wollte die Gedichte von Rilke haben. Ich freue mir immer dass er so bildungsdurstig ist. Werner lässt Dich tausendmal grüssen."

The description of this code was written in shorthand on a little slip of thin paper, and I was to give this secretly to Hans as I greeted him. This difficult and dangerous task made me very nervous. In the train I felt as if I was being watched, and I quite expected to see Marowski get into the train at one of the stations. When I got out a woman left the train who had regarded me with great interest during the journey; and I saw her disappear into the prison building.

I had to wait outside the gate for an hour before I was taken to Hans. I thought to myself: if anyone were to see me pass the note to Hans the consequences would be disastrous to him, and I should be cut off from him altogether. But even if he gets it safely he will have to decipher the note. And while he does so the prisoner who shares the cell with him may be watching him. And this man doesn't look very trustworthy.

The longer I stood there the crazier the whole plan seemed. The very fact that I had the note on my person filled me with terror. But I had not the courage to tear it up and throw the fragments away. I put it into my mouth, and I felt desperate when I realized how long I should have to chew it before I could swallow it.

At last the note had safely reached my stomach. But what was I to do now? Hans must have a code, and I did not dare to go home without giving him one. And it was such a difficult code: Heinz and Margot had spent a long time thinking it out. I found it difficult enough to explain the code in cold blood; how could I convey it to Hans in a disguised form? My brain was whirling with the effort. Nothing whatever had occurred to me when I was taken to see Hans.

But necessity is the mother of invention, stimulating the mind to more than its normal ingenuity. I bent over

Hans, who was lying in bed, for he was still very weak, and as I gave him the usual kiss of greeting I murmured in his ear: "D = E, E = N, N = K." He looked at me as though he thought I had become insane, and I myself did not know how to continue. I sat beside his bed and stroked his hand.

The pleasant orderly had never objected to this. As a preliminary, I always exhibited both hands in a purely official gesture, to show that I had nothing concealed in them; and on this occasion I even laid my handbag out of reach. On my first visit the orderly had given a warning: "Never try to pass anything to your son. I should have to report it, and then you would never see him again." So on each visit I showed him, by this gesture of the hands, that I had not forgotten his advice.

I began: "I have something absurd that I must tell you to-day: it will amuse you. Our friend Curt is writing a book on *Die Denkmalsfigur*."

"What!" said Hans. "Is he crazy?"

"That's what I asked him," I said, "and I told him that I regarded the title, *Denkmalsfigur*, and the whole sub-ject, as a topical theme, quite unworthy of such a schol-arly writer. But he insists that the title, *Denkmalsfigur*, is a perfectly objective, historical title, and that the work is completely in accordance with his own speciality."

Each time the word *Denkmalsfigur* was spoken my stroking fingers exerted a sudden pressure, and on the first repetition Hans realized that I had something of im-

portance to communicate.   From his strained expression
I knew that his mind was busily at work.

"Curt says," I continued, "that this work of his on the
Denkmalsfigur will deal exclusively with Gothic problems; and indeed, that every fourth word would be
Gothic."   (At "fourth word" I pressed his hand again.)
Hans was evidently thinking hard.   He had not the least
idea of my intention, but he began of his own accord to
enlarge upon the subject.   "Yes, I can very well imagine
him writing about the Bamberg and Magdeburg equestrian monuments."

"Yes," I said.   "He has discovered four especially fine
equestrian statues of this period [at 'four' another pressure of the fingers], and he promised to give me the four
photographs for you, as he thought you would have more
understanding for such work than I."

At this moment the orderly was called to the door, but
he did not actually leave the room.   I whispered, almost
inaudibly, but so that he could read my lips: $D = E$,
$E = N$, $N = K$, $K = M$, $M = A$."   By this time the
orderly was back at his post, but my son's expression suddenly relaxed.   He burst out laughing, and said: "Give
Curt my very best wishes, tell him that I understand what
he is driving at, and that I should very much like to hear
more about it."

The next letter from Hans contained a message in the
smuggled code.

CHAPTER V

The Minister for Justice is Powerless

HANS WAS NOT recovering his strength. He was still weak from the loss of blood, in spite of the intravenous injections. The poison had injured his stomach, and the constant examinations upset him, so that he brought up all that he swallowed.

This, we thought, was just as well; for we knew what would happen as soon as he was strong enough to leave the infirmary: he would go back to the camp or the Gestapo, perhaps to be tortured again. We advised him, in code messages, to take as little food as possible; for his weakness was his safeguard. He replied, also in code, that he could not fast without being detected; for a strict account was kept of all that he ate, and all that he brought up again.

I called on Dr. Schlegel and begged him to consider the state of my son's nerves; the constant examinations were extremely bad for him. Dr. Schlegel replied that he could not help that. My son was in a very nasty situation, and it wasn't to be wondered at if his nerves gave way. However, he was no fool. He knew what he had to do to help himself.   He had apparently made things better for himself in Spandau when he began to find things too intolerable.

When I indignantly told him what had happened there (in order to explain my son's attempted suicide), he behaved as though he had absolutely no knowledge of the matter; but he did at least promise me that he would not discharge Hans from the infirmary until he was in a better state of health.

Since I saw that there was nothing to be done with Schlegel I looked up various nerve-doctors with a view to obtaining a certificate as to my son's nervous condition. They must, of course, be reputable doctors who often had to state their opinions in writing, or who are actually attached to a prison as specialists in nervous diseases. Some of these, I found, were Jews, who were therefore out of the question.

Bonhöfer seemed to me a likely man, since it was he who was consulted in respect of van der Lubbe.   He explained that he could give a certificate of the kind I wanted only if such were required by the authorities. But he gave me the names of various forensic physicians, including that of Dr. Störmer, a man with all sorts of useful connections.

Störmer was extremely nice to me, but he declared that it was impossible that such things as I had described could ever happen.   It had always been his experience that in the case of the slightest brutality the guilty official was dismissed, or at all events very severely punished. (Quite a number of sensible doctors and lawyers continued for months, and even for years, to believe that they were still living in a legal and constitutional State.) So, even if there had just for once been a little trouble, such a thing would certainly not occur a second time.

"Then how do you explain my son's condition?"

"I expect he is suffering from a prison psychosis."

That was just what I had wanted him to say.

"Of course, you can judge better than I. But it must be a very severe prison psychosis. I am sure you will consider, after you have examined him, that he ought to go to a psychopathic institute. For if the troubles of which my son complains are merely nervous phenomena one would really have to say that such a degree of nervousness amounted to insanity. For in that case a blinded eye, a damaged auditory canal, a broken leg, a fractured jaw, and a number of broken teeth are not the results of brutal maltreatment, but of sheer nervousness!"

"No, that they can't be. Such conditions cannot result from neurasthenia."

"But these conditions are present. Some I have seen with my own eyes, others are admitted by the doctors in charge of the case. How do you explain that if they are due neither to brutality nor to neurasthenia?"

Of course, he could not explain them. He advised me to go to the Gestapo and to tell them that I was rather uneasy. They would, of course, be perfectly nice to me;

they would ring up the infirmary, and matters would be as I wished.

"You accursed idiot!" The words escaped me, despite myself; they were spoken loudly and distinctly. But he was so engrossed in his rosy and sentimental description of the Gestapo's benevolence that they passed unnoticed, and he adjured me always to come to him if I should have any further anxieties.

So I gave up my dreams of a psychopathic institute; the more readily as various experts assured me that under the present Government the change would not necessarily be for the better.

Through von Blomberg I obtained an interview with the Minister for Justice, Gürtner. In the waiting-room a secretary told me that the Minister was receiving me in the interval between two important conferences, and that he had very little time to spare. He himself would be glad to avoid the painful necessity of interrupting a lady's conversation, so he begged me to prepare myself for this interview by a consultation with an advocate (as I should have to speak of all sorts of legal matters of which I knew nothing). He advised me to express myself as briefly as possible, and finally to give Gürtner a very concisely written synopsis, so that he would not have to burden his memory with details. This written synopsis comprised a statement of the facts (the application of torture to extort a false deposition, etc.), with a request that examinations of this kind should be prohibited, and that my son should be allowed to employ an advocate in whom he had confidence. It was evident that the fact that I expressed myself so concisely, and with such technical accuracy, made a very good impression on Gürtner. When I had finished he said: "I should like you to let me have a written statement of all that you have told me"; upon which, as though it were the most natural thing in the world, I handed him the desired statement. He was visibly surprised by this prompt despatch.

He asked me a question: "What was your actual reason for applying to me? After all, Frank and Freisler[1] would be competent to deal with your case."

"I had three reasons," I explained. "Firstly, I could hardly have obtained an interview with Herr Frank or Herr Freisler, as I am in touch only with the German Nationalists, but not with the National Socialists. Secondly, I have more confidence in you than in these two gentlemen; and thirdly, I think it very important that the Minister for Justice should learn, for once, how justice is administered in the Third Reich, for, after all, he is really responsible for its administration."

He looked at me quietly; he was neither vexed nor

[1] Dr. Hans Frank (born 1900), in 1933 Bavarian Minister for Justice and Commissioner of Justice for the Reich; later, Reich Minister without portfolio and Commissioner for the *Gleichchaltung* (making uniform) of the Justice of the States and for the *Erneuerung* (renewal) of the laws. Dr. Roland Freisler (born 1893), Secretary of State in the Reich Ministry of Justice and Prussian Councillor of State.

surprised. "I understand your reasons. I will forward your application with a recommendation to the competent authority."

And with that the interview ended, within fifteen minutes, as he had wished.

A week later, as I had received no reply, I rang up Gürtner's secretary. He assured me that he had forwarded my petition with Gürtner's recommendation. He promised to remind his chief of the matter. He promised as much on two further occasions. Then he told me that they could do nothing more. What lay in their power to do they had done.

I heard afterwards from friends of Gürtner's that he had followed my son's case with the keenest interest, but that he was unable to do anything for him.

In the Ministry for Justice, as in the Reichswehr Ministry, the aristocratic atmosphere, the silence, and the courteous treatment received from all, from the porter to the Minister, impressed me most agreeably. How different things were in the Gestapo! There everything was always in an uproar, thanks to the noisy and loutish behaviour of the swarms of men coming off duty. In the rooms where the relatives of men under "protective arrest" had to give their names there was a constant flow of bad language. Many of these people were never announced at all, and there were always sad and anxious faces.

Once I met a woman there who was leaving the town

without having obtained an interview. She was crying bitterly, and was followed by the curses and abuse of the man to whom she had appealed. An SA man asked him: "What have you been up to with her?" This was his reply: "The carrion can't open her mouth enough to say 'Heil Hitler,' so I gave her what for. She'll learn soon enough."

I myself could not open my mouth wide enough; hitherto I had got off with a silent lifting of the arm. After this I always opened it when I visited the office of the Gestapo or any other premises of the kind. But although I did my best to speak the words quietly and inconspicuously, it always sounded like a war-cry, and the person thus greeted always looked at me with a startled expression; except that Captain H., who was so kind to me later on, used to smile amiably when I roared the words "Heil Hitler" at him, responding with a friendly "Heil Hitler, gracious lady!" If I ventured to omit the greeting he would say, still pleasantly, but in a tone of distinct admonition, "Heil Hitler, gracious lady!" and smiling his acknowledgment of my war-cry: "Heil Hitler, Herr Hauptmann!"

The men of the Gestapo did not exactly shout at me, but they were not amiable. Above all, there was always a prolonged dispute before they would announce me. I sometimes had to talk to them for half an hour before they consented to do so, and on such occasions I was no more amiable than they. Once, when Conrady gave me an appointment, I said. "Please give me that in writing." He looked astonished. "But that is really superfluous!"—"No, unfortunately it isn't at all superfluous. Every time you have made an appointment by telephone I have had a long fight with these people. They ask me for written evidence that you have really given me an appointment. And now that I am speaking of the matter, I ought to tell you that the tone of these men downstairs is abominable. They treat me as though I were a troublesome beggar. I am not a supplicant, I am a human being contending for her rights, and I ask that I should be treated accordingly."

"I will give orders," he replied, "that you shall have no trouble in future."

And from that day my treatment was irreproachable. The men seemed to bear me no grudge for my complaint; but the tone of their behaviour to the other applicants did not seem to improve.

I never felt really at ease during my visits to the Gestapo and the Ministry. Hitherto I had seldom had any experience of the seamy side of life. My husband had always insisted that it was a husband's duty to shield his wife from the asperities of life. If I sometimes went a little too far my husband's position protected me; indeed, thanks to this position I could do or say things which would have given offence in other people, but which in me were described as original or perfectly delightful. But now I had no such protection. If I took a false step I might do untold harm. Whom could I find to advise me? We had not been living very long in Berlin, and I felt that the majority of my friends were unqualified to help me. I must find someone in a position of authority, who knew from his own experience how one should deal with such people as I had to meet. And he must be absolutely reliable. I looked up some friends of my husband's; they behaved splendidly to me, although I hardly knew them, and although any intercourse with me was bound to cause them great anxiety. Some of them had lost their positions in the Ministries, either because they were Jews, or because their opinions were heretical. They always found time to see me; and they always knew just which influential people would be helpful, and which must be avoided. They saw to it that my applications and inquiries were expressed in the proper form, and not in such a way as to give offence.

One of these friends said one day: "I really don't know why I should advise you so carefully. After all, when you have an interview with anyone you always do the precise opposite of what we had agreed you should do, and I always find afterwards that you have taken just the right steps, with the certainty of a sleepwalker!"

But I felt very much safer when I set out with precise instructions, so the anxious consultations were continued. Despite my somnambulistic certainty, my friend was apparently by no means confident that I should walk delicately enough, for whenever I had a particularly difficult interview either he or his wife would look me up in the afternoon, in order to make sure that I had really returned safely.

One friend of mine, in a position of considerable influence, who had done all that he could, without himself being liquidated, to stop certain Nazi brutalities, put me in touch with some of the leading Nazi jurists. I was therefore able to give certain valuable information to Gürtner.

My friend held the opinion that we could not induce Gürtner to take steps that would endanger his position. He was the one person who could take legal steps to prevent the very worst from happening. Gürtner, for example, was the only man who had tried to prevent the imposition of the death-sentence for "racial defilement"; and this on the grounds that such a law would be too damaging to the reputation of Germany in foreign countries. He utterly repudiated my own view that the people who co-operated with such a gangster Government, even if by so doing they prevented "the very worst" from happening, became its accomplices.

Thanks to his introduction I obtained an interview with Freisler. He was really the only one among the higher officials who treated me with impertinence. When I had spoken in vindication of my son, he exclaimed: "Of course, that's all absolutely untrue. How can you say that your son was actuated by idealism! I've got the documents here." (An official stood beside him, all this time, in a reverential attitude, holding the documents open for inspection.) "For his part in the Felseneck trial your son received from the *Rote Hilfe* alone the sum of—." I forgot how many marks, but it was a very small amount.

"That," I replied, "confirms what I have said; the sum is so ridiculously small! He worked day and night in connection with that trial, so that he could not touch any other business."

Freisler once more named the sum, in a wrathful tone, and brought his fist down on the documents. "Here it is, so you can't say that your son worked without pay!"

"I tell you," I replied, "that he was a loser by the trial. After all, you have been an advocate yourself; you know how high overhead expenses are. After my son was arrested I had to pay a large sum in settlement of unpaid rent. His secretary has told me that during this trial he could not accept any other business, and that he had to engage an assistant to attend to the cases already in hand; and my son had to pay him more than he made over the Felseneck trial. And the overhead expenses were still mounting up. There was absolutely nothing left for his personal expenses. The official counsel for the defence in the Felseneck trial did well out of it, but my son spent his little savings on it, ran into debt, and worked himself almost to death. Can you deny that he acted out of sheer idealism?"

"In my eyes," retorted Friesler, "he is a man absolutely

without conscience, for whom I should not under any circumstances lift a finger."

"Then," I said, "I can do no good here. I am sorry I came to you. Good-bye."

Nevertheless, Freisler did appeal to Hitler, and actually put in a word for my son. He told his friends afterwards: "No one will be able to do anything for Litten. Hitler went purple in the face when he heard his name."

And then I appealed to the Crown Prince. I rang him up at Potsdam. He could not receive me, as he was ill in bed; but I was to see his adjutant.

This officer was all amiability. He was sorry to hear that my husband was abroad; Her Majesty the Empress Hermine was in Berlin, and was holding a reception. He had been on the point of sending my husband an invitation. I had the impression that he found it very painful that a member of such a family as ours should be guilty of defending Communists.

He suggested that I could speak to him without reserve, as whatever the Crown Prince did would be done through him. But he could not promise me that anything would come of it; for the Crown Prince himself was absolutely powerless nowadays.

Was he—I asked—aware of the state of popular feeling? It seemed to me significant that when the Crown Prince appeared on the screen in a news reel he received more applause than the Führer of the Third Reich.

He smiled: "Of course, we are not unaware of these things."

"Then the Führer too must know them," I said. "Don't you think that a man who is so beloved by the nation might have just a little influence with the Führer?"

"His Imperial Highness," objected the adjutant, "has to be extremely cautious."

"You can't mean by that," I exclaimed, "that his Imperial Highness would be afraid to intervene on my son's behalf? I simply cannot imagine that a Hohenzollern would be afraid."

"Of course not; you are right there. And he will try to do something for your son. But I can't imagine that he will be able to do any good."

I had a definite impression that nothing would be done.

Not long after this I heard from certain East Prussian nobles (many of whom were of course on terms of friendship with the Crown Prince, regarding him, or at all events his eldest son, as their future ruler) that the Crown Prince was supposed to have intervened with Hitler on my son's behalf; and that Hitler had shouted at him: "Anyone who intervenes on Litten's behalf goes straight into camp, even if it's yourself!"

Whether that is true I have never been able to discover.

Of these East Prussian nobles a number endeavoured

to use their influence on Hans' behalf. I remember, for example, that Graf G. once came to see me as he was passing through Berlin, and invited me to accompany him to the Herren-Klub; he would see if anything could be done through Papen. We decided that he had better go without me, in order to reconnoitre, while I waited where he could quickly find me. However, he found that his friends of the Herren-Klub were reluctant to have any dealings with me, as the consequences might be unpleasant for them. They promised to take certain steps, but at the moment my son's situation was apparently so much more favourable (this was during his second term in Spandau) that they thought it better to avoid causing irritation by doing anything that was not absolutely necessary.

And here I ought to place it on record that many of the East Prussian Junkers were far more loyal and courageous than some of our other friends. During the more recent years of the Nazi régime one or another of them would always come to see my husband if he was passing through Berlin. Not one of them had any sympathy with the Third Reich; but on their estates they were less molested and less closely observed than the rest of our acquaintances. Those who held official posts had, of course, to be particularly cautious.

I had been told that Hitler had a high appreciation of Furtwängler, and was on terms of friendship with him;

and that Furtwängler, although a Nazi, was always ready
to help others. I sent him an urgent message, asking for
a few minutes' conversation. He was very busy at the
time, and gave me an appointment at the opera. I had
to wait in his room until there was a break in the re-
hearsal which he was conducting.

When I told him what had been happening he strode
excitedly to and fro, exclaiming indignantly: "What has
become of humanity?" Then he asked me, in some surprise, what had given me the idea of appealing to him of
all persons? I told him what I had heard of his friendship with Hitler, and of his kindness; and I continued:
"Of course, I am doing an unconventional thing in appealing to the kindness of a perfect stranger. And in
order to explain why I am doing so I am obliged to say
something that is, I am afraid, in doubtful taste. I am
convinced that so great an artist as yourself must also be
a great man. And of such a man one can expect that in
an exceptional case he may take an unusual step."

He nodded; apparently he did not find my remark in
bad taste. "Yes, I might, I might. And it is true that I
like to help others, but the people I help are always
members of my own profession; for example, I try to
ensure that a musician is not thrown out of employment.
I have often been able to help in that way. But a political case? I should be told: 'Cobbler, stick to your last!
Don't meddle in political affairs of which you know
nothing!'"

"Do you call it a political affair if one tries to save a human being from torture? I think that is a matter of mere humanity. And anyone who esteems a man as an artist will surely allow him to defend the cause of humanity."

"Yes," said Furtwängler, thoughtfully, "perhaps it could be done. Yes, I'll do it. I promise you that I'll try. I'll speak first of all to Hitler's adjutant, Brükner; I can see him at any time."

Furtwängler's secretary rang me up a few times. He begged me not to be impatient; things were not going so quickly as he had hoped; and the next message was that the matter was more difficult than he had imagined; it would be very difficult indeed to do anything.

It was always the same story, however anxious people were to help me.

CHAPTER VI

Brandenburg: "The Prisoners Shall Pay for This!"

AFTER OUR FIRST VISIT to the infirmary Conrady had forbidden Margot to visit Hans again. However, the second time I went to see him she managed to smuggle herself in. At her request I contrived to look as old and fragile as possible, so that the doorkeeper allowed her to accompany me to the door of the ward. The orderly upstairs, who was present at our interviews, unsuspectingly admitted her. But Conrady apparently heard of the matter, and when next I saw him he informed me that if Frau Fürst accompanied me again without a permit I should not be allowed to visit my son again.

When I told Margot this, she replied: "Then I'll marry him. They can't refuse to let his wife visit him!" And her husband agreed: "If it will help Hans, by all means!"

In the meanwhile Margot had discovered that one could apply directly to the Moabit Infirmary for permits, and that the official whose business it was to issue them was not particularly strict. She duly applied for a permit for herself.

But when she presented herself on the following day the official regretted to inform her that he would have to cancel the permit, as Litten had just been discharged from the infirmary. She questioned him urgently, and learned that he was to be sent to the Columbia House; in fact, they would be coming for him at any moment.

Margot, in a state of great excitement, hurried off to find me. She had paid a flying call on one of Hans' former clients, who had a great affection for him. He placed himself and his car at my disposal for the day. We knew that haste was essential, and that it would be an exhausting day. Schlegel had broken his promise. He had allowed Hans to be discharged from the infirmary although he was still weak and shaking, and although he was still bringing up all that he swallowed.

To begin with, I rang up the Gestapo. Neither Conrady nor Diels was accessible. Blomberg was attending a conference, and his adjutant was sure that he would not be available for some hours. Apart from that, Herr von Blomberg could not help me. I must have read the decree in the newspapers, that officials within whose competence such matters did not lie were not allowed to concern themselves with the affairs of persons under preventive detention.

The decree was inspired by class feeling. It was contrary to the Nazi *Weltanschauung* that people of "good family" should use their personal influence for the benefit of internees of their own class. No one did anything to help the workers. There must be equal justice for all!

"What shall I do, then?"

"Apply direct to Göring's adjutant. Göring is the competent authority."

I was afraid Göring's adjutant would not receive me without an introduction; but Blomberg's adjutant assured me that he himself would ask him to see me.

When I had told Göring's young adjutant what I had come for, and had begged him to rescue Hans from the Columbia House, he asked me: "But, gracious lady, do you really believe that the Prime Minister of all people will help a Communist?"

I banged on the table with my fist and shouted at him. "I am convinced of one thing, at all events. These gentry are always speaking of German honour. And if Herr Göring cares anything for German honour he must realize that there must be an end of such cases as this. For all these things that are constantly happening, and in particular this case of my son, are such that a dog might well refuse to take a crust from the hand of a German! That is what our German honour has come to!"

He turned pale and sprang to his feet. "Now," I thought, "I shall be arrested!" But to my astonishment he exclaimed: "Yes, you are right!" and ran out of the room. Presently he returned, saying: "I have just been talking to Dr. Diels (leader of the Gestapo) over the telephone. He has promised me that he will fetch your son from the Columbia House immediately, without previous notice, and will have him sent on to Spandau."

I should explain that I had proposed that he should then and there drive to the Columbia House with me, so that I myself could remove my son. When he laughed at the idea, saying that I must surely see that it was impossible, I said: "That sounds very curious to me. But what if these people are simply told to take my son elsewhere, and beat him to death before the order can be executed? I have heard of such cases before now." This was why he had arranged that Diels should give no warning of his arrival.

Finally, he told me in confidence that Herr von Blomberg, when he was rung up, had taken pains to make it clear that he was not in the least interested in my son's case. This shocking behaviour on the part of a man who had hitherto been so chivalrous was explained by those who knew by the fact that by this time Blomberg's own position was insecure. But from this time onwards he seemed to become—shall I say, cautious?—in his behaviour to other acquaintances who were far less "unreliable" than I.

An hour later—for I estimated that the journey would take an hour—I rang up Spandau to ask if my son had arrived yet. I was told that he was not there, and could not be received there, as persons under protective detention were no longer being sent to Spandau.

I rang up my own apartment, to explain why I had

been so long, and I was told that an express letter from Hans had been delivered, in which he said that he was going to be sent away, he did not know where, and I must do everything possible to prevent it. The delivery of this letter told me that there was at least one kindly person in the infirmary.

I rang up Moabit immediately. A voice that sounded rather confused and embarrassed explained that it was impossible to give me any information over the telephone. We drove to Moabit, and managed to obtain an interview with some very decent officials, who told us that an order had been received to the effect that Litten was to be taken to the Columbia House. At the last moment, however, this order had been cancelled (no doubt as the result of my interview with Göring's adjutant), and they were now waiting for further orders. The official who told me this promised to give Hans a note in which I told him that I had been running about all day to do what I could for him, and that I hoped it would prove that I had been successful.

Next morning Margot went to Moabit again, where the kindly official told her, in the strictest confidence, that Hans had been taken to Brandenburg. Once more I rang up Conrady, who insisted that he had no information. I exclaimed that it was a scandal that a man so seriously ill should be sent back to camp already. He promised me that Hans should be sent, if not to a hospital, at all events to a camp infirmary.

"I know," I said, "that my son is no longer in the infirmary, and I have the feeling that you have sent him to Brandenburg, and that is a camp which has a particularly bad reputation."

He was extremely anxious to know how I had learned that Hans was in Brandenburg.

"I hit on Brandenburg by chance," I said. "But in any case, I know it's a ghastly place."

I could get nothing out of him, except that when my son had reached his destination he would send me his address.

A few days later I did receive a letter from Hans; the new address was—Brandenburg. He also told me, in code: "I am brutally ill-treated hourly."

Again I spoke to Conrady over the telephone. I reproached him bitterly for breaking his promise that Hans should be taken to the camp infirmary, and I told him that I had definite information that my son was being ill-treated. He laughed at me, but refused to give me a visitor's permit. This would be issued only after the prisoner had been some time in the camp.

In his next letter Hans asked me to send him a pair of buckled shoes, as they were not allowed to wear laced boots or shoes. What was the meaning of this prohibition? Was it more red tape, or were they afraid that a prisoner might strangle himself with his boot-laces?

I went to Brandenburg, but I was sent away without seeing my son; I could not even interview the commandant. I wrote to the commandant, saying that I absolutely must speak to him, and asking him to appoint a date for a visit. He replied that he was so busy that he could not make a definite appointment, and it would be annoying for me if he made an appointment and was then unable to receive me. So I should have to take my chance.

In the meantime I received another letter from Hans, in which he spoke of terrible ill-treatment. And again he asked for poison: for cyanide of potassium, and plenty of it. We were to send him a suit of clothes, having sewn the poison into the lining of the right sleeve under the padding of the shoulder.

It was a week before we could procure the poison. The young chemist who had helped us before had to steal it; there was no other way of obtaining it.

To sew it into the lining in an unobtrusive fashion was more difficult that I had imagined. After I had spent some hours on unsuccessful efforts I took the jacket to the wife of a reliable client, who was herself a dressmaker. She sewed the poison up in a long strip of cambric, so that nothing could be felt or seen; but the jacket smelt strongly of prussic acid, which no amount of airing would remove. Any intelligent searcher would know at once what was hidden in the jacket; and if the poison were discovered all communication with the camp would be broken off. We dared not send it. Hans realized this, and as in the meanwhile conditions had improved we postponed the attempt until we could hit on some less conspicuous method.

Later on, when he had been removed to the Lichtenburg camp, where he was comfortable, we were thankful that we had failed. And his friends believed that he was still destined for great things, because all his attempts to take his own life were unsuccessful.

Once more, with considerable difficulty, I obtained an interview with Dr. Conrady, and I told him roundly that I knew for certain that my son was being ill-treated.

"Did you learn that from your son's letters?" he asked.

"His letters tell me nothing; there is really nothing in them. That alone is a proof that things are going badly with him."

"But you must have received information somehow, since you make such a positive statement."

"No," I replied, "I have not received any definite information; but I am clairvoyant."

He stared at me for a while with a puzzled expression; this brazen effrontery was too much for him. "Do you believe in that sort of thing?" he asked me at last.

"Not in the least," I replied, "but I do sometimes see things."

I told him of a few of my past experiences, and in particular of my experience in connection with the apprentice whom the SA men had murdered. I declared that the same smell of blood which I had noticed then was now emitted by my son's letters.

He looked thoughtful at this; apparently he was trying to decide whether I was a shameless liar or whether there was perhaps some truth in what I said. At last he exclaimed: "Well, you can't possibly expect me to go into such matters."

"I don't," I replied. "I only wanted to explain how I obtained the information, as this seemed to interest you so. But I do expect you to make an inquiry into the matter."

"Your son," said Conrady, "is so hated by the SS that one needn't be surprised if he is roughly handled. After all, I can't always be everywhere."

"That," I replied, "is what Dr. S. said when my son was maltreated at Sonnenburg. But he did do what I asked; he took my son away."

Conrady showed his teeth as he answered me. "I shan't do *that*," he said. And I knew he was thinking: Yes, and that cost him his post!

"If I were in your place," I cried, "I would soon restore order in the camp, even if I couldn't always be everywhere!"

"Oh, what would you do if you were in my place?"

"I would hold an inquiry," I said, "and I would see to it that the first man who was convicted of ill-treating prisoners was shot. If that didn't stop it I would have ten shot. And if even that was ineffective," I continued, exasperated by his scornful smile, "I would hang up five hundred of them, all round the camp, and leave them to rot and stink. You could be quite sure that that would be effective."

He stroked his throat uneasily, as though he saw himself dangling. Then he laughed again—that cold, scornful laugh.

Next day I received an anonymous letter, written on a typewriter. "Dear Frau Litten, your son is being tortured daily in the Brandenburg concentration camp. We know that you have distinguished connections. Why are you doing nothing to help Litten? Are you too timid, or don't you know what is on everyone's lips?"

I thought then, and I think now, that this letter was written by friends who wanted to give me a pretext for taking further steps, and to furnish me with "evidence" of a sort. But I never learned the identity of the writer.

However, I rang up Conrady, and when I heard that he was away on official business I sent the letter to the leader of the Gestapo, Dr. Diels, since he would neither come to the telephone nor consent to see me. I begged him to hold an immediate inquiry into the conditions obtaining in Brandenburg.

That same day I drove to Brandenburg and asked to see the commandant. I explained that he had told me to come "at a venture." They laughed at me. "I am going to sit here," I said, "and I shall not move until I have spoken to the commandant. If he doesn't come to-day I shall sit here again to-morrow. And I shall do this until I have spoken to him."

After some time a man appeared who described himself as representing the commandant. I merely told him, "I must speak to the commandant himself!" The result of my obstinacy was that about an hour later the commandant made his appearance. I handed him a copy of the anonymous letter. He roared at me: "You are really absolutely shameless! How dare you come here with such things! It's a libel to say that such a thing could happen in my camp!"

"I quite agree with you," I said. "I consider that it reflects upon your personal honour, but I think you should be grateful to me for calling your attention to the matter, so that you can hold an inquiry and stop anything of the kind."

He shouted again: "I shall not dream of holding an inquiry! Such things simply don't happen!"

"But of course such things happen," I replied. "I have already heard of such things in other camps, and I was able to adduce evidence that they had happened. At the Gestapo they quite openly admitted that such things have happened. Why should it be impossible for them to occur in your camp?"

"Other camps," he roared, "are no concern of mine. But this concerns my camp. And I have no intention of holding an inquiry."

After some hesitation, he said in conclusion: "As far as I am concerned you are welcome to see your son. Then he can tell you himself that he's all right."

"I am very grateful to you," I said. "But of course I must ask you to let me see him alone. He will never tell me the truth before a guard."

"That again is sheer presumption. You know perfectly well that all conversations with prisoners must take place in the presence of a guard."

"And you know just as well that my son can't talk reasonably in front of a guard. For example, the guard might be one of the very men who have ill-treated him."

"Very well!" said the commandant. "Then I will be present at your interview myself!"

I could make no objection to this, and thankfully accepted his offer.

I was told later on by a discharged prisoner that the commandant had asked my son: "Litten, are you going to tell your mother that you have been maltreated?"—"No."—"Are you going to tell her that you are well treated?"—"Yes"—"Then you can see her."

Hans appeared in the charge of the commandant. He looked dreadful; his eyes were like those of a hunted animal, and there were bright red streaks round his throat, which were barely concealed by a muffler.

"I was very anxious to speak to you," I explained, "because I've received an anonymous letter which has made me very uneasy."

"Yes, I've heard of that letter," said Hans, with exaggerated cheerfulness. "How could you believe such nonsense? I'm extremely comfortable here."

"All the same," I objected, "I don't think you look at all well. I feel very worried about your health. You were very ill indeed when you were discharged from the hospital. Apparently Dr. Conrady's promise that you should be placed in the sick-ward here was not kept."

The commandant offered an explanation: "We had no idea what was the matter with your son, and at first we let him work like the rest. But as soon as we saw that he wasn't well he was treated with the greatest of care." And turning to my son with an amiable smile: "That is so, isn't it? You are very comfortable now, aren't you?"

"Yes, I am very comfortable."

"Then why," I demanded, "is your throat covered with red streaks?"

"You know," said Hans, "how clumsy I am when I shave myself. I have cut myself over and over again."

"I was told by a discharged prisoner," I said, "that your work here consisted in lying on the floor of the courtyard and scratching out the earth between the flag-stones with your finger-nails."

"How can you believe such nonsense?" cried Hans, quickly.

"Well, just let me see your hands. How is it that your nails are so preposterously short? They never used to be like that!"

My son's beautifully shaped finger-nails looked as though they had been gnawed away.

"Oh," said Hans, "don't be so absurd. I cut my nails this morning, and they've come out rather short."

"What is your work, then?" I asked.

The commandant began to bluster again. "Now I've had enough of your stupid questions! That'll do!" And my son was led away.

During the interview I had observed both Hans and the commandant very closely, and at one moment, when the commandant had turned to me with an amiable smile, in order to convince me that my son was being most carefully treated, Hans had pointed to him with such a terrible expression on his face that I understood in a flash: "This commandant is the biggest brute in the camp!"

After Hans had been taken away, and while I was trying to thank the commandant amiably, he suddenly flushed purple with rage. Shaking his clenched fists, he snarled between his teeth: "The prisoners shall pay for this!"

My heart began to thump, I was so alarmed. I did my best to appease him; arguing that he positively must not vent his wrath on the unhappy prisoners. After all, they were not in the very least responsible for my attitude. It was quite possible, indeed, that they would strongly disapprove of it. If anyone was to blame it was myself alone. I was quite ready to apologize. As far as that went, I had convinced myself that all these rumours were nonsensical. My son himself had contradicted them.

And the way in which the commandant had spoken to my son had been altogether charming, and had shown me how kindly he treated the prisoners. He definitely ought to realize that my visit could only be beneficial and in the interest of all. Now I could contradict the non-sensical rumours which were flying about.

In my desperate state of mind I said anything that entered my head.

I did really manage to appease him, and we parted on friendly terms.

I felt utterly exhausted: I felt that I had committed a folly, and that the prisoners would suffer for it. Somehow, at all costs, I must put things right.

Dr. Conrady was back again, but he had the reputation of never consenting to see the relatives of persons under "protective arrest." It had always taken me a long time to persuade him to grant me an interview. I rang him up now:

"Dr. Conrady, I must speak to you at once; I have the evidence you wanted in respect of the Brandenburg camp."

This interested him. "Come at once," he replied.

Half an hour later I was in his office. First, without a word, I passed him a copy of the anonymous letter. He read it, turned it about, and held it up to the light. I interrupted him:

"Don't bother to examine that; it's written on my notepaper with my typewriter." He looked at me in bewilderment. "I have naturally sent the original to Dr. Diels; that is a copy which I made myself."

He laughed angrily. "Do you know that they suspect you here of writing the letter yourself?"

"But why in all the world," I cried, "should I hide myself behind an anonymous letter? I am constantly speaking my mind to you much more plainly than anything is expressed in this letter."

"That," he admitted, "is just what I said. But as far as that goes, we soon discovered the writer."

I was startled. "Who is it?"

"Why does that interest you so?"

"Because I am sorry for these people," I said, "and because I have apparently done a very foolish thing. I thought it would be impossible to discover the writer of a typewritten letter. At all events, it cannot have been a friend of mine."

"Oh? Why not?"

"Do you really believe that anyone who knows me personally would reproach me with cowardice?"

He had to laugh at that. Not long after this the Fürsts' typewriter was confiscated, so I concluded that they had not discovered the writer.

"Well," I said, "I have brought you the evidence you wanted. But before I say anything I must have your word of honour that nothing unpleasant happens to the person who furnished it."

"You can't possibly ask me to give you my word of honour," he said.

"Why not?" I inquired. "I can tell you nothing until I have it. Unless you give me your word of honour I haven't, unfortunately, the least confidence that you would leave the person in question unmolested."

"Frau Litten," he complained, "what a way of addressing an official! I have never known anything like it!"

"You really mustn't be angry with me," I said. "I have never before in my life had any dealings with officials, except in society. I think they would all tell you, if you inquired, that I was always perfectly correct in my behaviour, and particularly amiable. But as regards any official dealings with them I have as yet no experience. You must simply tell me how I ought to behave."

Conrady was somewhat appeased by this. "You really must see for yourself, Frau Litten, that things can't go on like this. You are constantly scolding me and cross-examining me. Now you actually ask me to give you my word of honour."

"Then please tell me," I said, "what I am to do in such a situation. You ask me for evidence; but without your word of honour I can't give you my evidence. What am I to do?"

"Why," said Conrady, in a tone of kindly persuasion, "just fire away and tell me all you know. You have had news from the camp?"

"You know very well," I replied, "that if this is your attitude I cannot give you the evidence. But I will tell you about my visit to the camp. I spoke to the commandant yesterday, and they brought out my son to see me. And both the commandant and my son himself assured me that he was going on splendidly."

"Then what do you want?" Conrady asked. "The commandant is a reliable man, well on in years; a man in a high position, with many war decorations."

"I wasn't looking at his shoulder-straps or his war decorations," I said. "I was looking at his face, and I can tell you this: the man is a beast!"

I described the whole of our interview, and I laid stress upon his remark: "The prisoners shall pay for this!"

Conrady suggested that I had been nervous; the commandant was really a charming fellow.

"If you really think that," I declared, "you know nothing whatever about human nature. And that, for a man in your position, is extremely regrettable! I see that I can't get justice from you." And then I lost control of myself. I said, slowly and distinctly, emphasizing each word separately: "The lowest, most cowardly, most dishonourable crime on earth is to maltreat a defenceless person; and"—pointing my finger at him—"the man who tolerates such behaviour is no better than the criminal himself."

He turned white as paper and sprang to his feet. "Now it's all up with me!" I thought. "But after the mischief I have done at the camp I must somehow induce him to intervene!" I had already found that when I could do nothing by being quiet and pleasant the most effective weapon was an outburst of wrath. I gave him no time to speak; I simply shouted: "I am going to get justice done somehow. I shall stop at nothing; I am afraid of nothing. And if I can't succeed at once I shall somehow make my way to Hitler and tell him of the crimes that are being committed in his State. But before I do that I will stand at the street corners and address the people."

Conrady had regained control of himself and was visibly amused. "I shouldn't advise you to do that. You would be arrested in five minutes at the latest."

"And then," I asked, "should I be prosecuted?"

"Of course."

"And then," I said, "should I be able to make in public and before the judges all my accusations against your camp? Then at last I should be able to bring about the investigation of the camp, which I can't get you to undertake."

"There you are mightily mistaken," said Conrady. "There would be no inquiry, and you would serve a long term of imprisonment for reporting atrocities of which you could not adduce proof."

"It is very decent to warn me," I said. "I don't yet understand the new justice. I am the wife of a jurist, so that I find the change over rather difficult. Of course, under these circumstances I shall take care to say nothing. I don't want to be imprisoned, because I want to fight for my son. At all events, I shall give you no excuse for imprisoning me. Of course, you can arrest me without legal excuse; you can torture me and beat me to death; I know that very well. But sooner or later you would have reason to wish that you hadn't. And I should rejoice at the scandal it would cause abroad. I am sorry I have been able to do nothing with you; but I don't allow myself to be beaten. Good-bye!"

"Frau Litten," said Conrady, "please be reassured; I give you my word that the maltreatment of your son shall cease."

"Now," I replied, "you yourself say that the maltreatment of my son shall cease. By that you confess that he has been maltreated."

"No, no!" cried Conrady. "When I said that I was only taking your point of view for the moment. I will take good care that your son shall not under any circumstances be maltreated again."

"Then I suppose I ought to go home full of gratitude, but unfortunately—I must say it—your promises do not in the least impress me. I have already received such promises from other persons, but they haven't made the very least difference. The people simply wanted to get rid of me."

"Do I seem to you as though my orders would not be obeyed?" asked Conrady.

I took a good look at him. "As a matter of fact," I said, "you don't. I have always had the impression that your subordinates are afraid of you. But I simply don't believe that you seriously want to stop this ill-treatment."

"Well, Frau Litten, I can only repeat my promise that the maltreatment shall cease."

In order to be just to the man, I must add that now and again Conrady was capable of a humane impulse. One day, when I had again been scolding him violently, and his eyes had their dangerous green glitter, I apologized: "You mustn't bear it against me when I speak so vehemently. But it is asking too much to expect that a mother should keep calm in the face of such happenings."

He bowed slightly. "If I were in such a situation," he said, "I should be fortunate if my mother were to take my part in just such a way."

Another day, when I had lost my temper, and abused the Gestapo in the most immoderate terms, he exclaimed, in a menacing tone: "Frau Litten, I admire your courage!"

"How do you know I have any courage?" I asked, in astonishment.

"It needs courage to say what you have just said to me."

"I have only told you the truth," I replied. "I have done that all my life, but I have never found that it needed courage. Does it need courage now, in the Third Reich, to tell the truth?"

"Your courage amazes me!" he said, in a still more menacing tone.

"And, of course, as a National Socialist you rejoice to see that a German woman has courage!" I retorted.

At this he rose to his feet and bowed. I accepted this as a gesture of farewell, and I took my leave hastily; I had no desire to test the possible consequences of his admiration.

As a matter of fact, the next letter from Hans contained a message in code saying that his situation had undergone a definite improvement. I assumed that Conrady had conveyed the promised order to the camp; whereas the prisoners concluded that my visit had had a good effect on the commandant. Probably both explanations were correct.

From Kurt Hiller I received a brief description of all that had been happening in Brandenburg. Prisoners who were employed in the office told him that an order had come from the Gestapo forbidding further maltreatment of Litten. From that time onwards the commandant was pleasant in his manner to Hans; he often spoke to him, and sometimes chatted with him. He told Hans, after my visit, that I had gone so far as to say things for which I might have got into trouble, but that he had been greatly impressed by my assurance.

From Hiller, too, I received a full description of the conditions then obtaining in Brandenburg. On the 24th October, 1933, he was sent there as one of a batch of prisoners. Brandenburg was an old prison which had been closed in the twenties, under Severing, as it did not satisfy the hygienic requirements. Now it was considered good enough for prisoners under "protective detention." Of these it contained about 1,100. Two prisoners were always confined in a single cell, but Hans was placed in solitary confinement, as no one was willing to share his cell. He was avoided like the plague by the other prisoners, as all knew that he was the object of especial hatred, and were afraid that by sharing his cell, or even by making his acquaintance, they might compromise themselves. This was naturally very depressing for Hans, the more so as among the new arrivals there were men with whom he was well acquainted, and to whom he had shown much kindness. Mühsam was treated in the same way.

The most shocking treatment was apparently reserved for newcomers. All were brutally maltreated. Moreover, they were forbidden to work in their cells, or to read; and these cells were unlit, so that they were in pitchy darkness from late in the afternoon until the next morning. They were given no water for washing or drinking, and they were not allowed to shave. Their jailers wanted these political prisoners to look as depraved as possible, so that they themselves might feel as depraved as possible.

The prisoners wore their own clothes. They had to run across the courtyards at racing speed. Those who lagged behind were shouted at, struck, and kicked. The dirtiest courtyard was chosen for exercising the prisoners. They were made to throw themselves flat and get up again, over and over again, to throw themselves down in puddles, to crawl through puddles some yards in length, to lie and rest in puddles. And this until they lost consciousness.

Hans, who was still in a condition of extreme debility, for he had bled himself white, and the poison had ruined his digestion, suffered from severe cardiac spasms and prolonged fainting-fits.

When they were not being exercised the prisoners were locked into their cells, where they spent their time in enforced idleness. Hans, however, was rarely left in peace; he was subjected to repeated questionings, with blows and torture, in respect of the Felseneck affair, and even the Reichstag fire, of which he had spoken to me in Moabit.

The prisoner who had been a fellow-patient in the Moabit hospital had thought to make things easier for himself by declaring that Hans had told him in confidence that van der Lubbe was a friend of his, and had taken refuge with him for some time before the fire. He gave a number of minute details, which sounded credible enough, as they were based on what he had read in the newspapers. Hans had no peace until the police discovered that van der Lubbe was actually in Holland when he was supposed to have been sleeping in my son's apartment.

I was told afterwards by Communists who had learned with dismay of these repeated questionings that not a single one of all the men whose activities were known to Hans was ever betrayed by him. They had only too often learned exactly how their party comrades had "bettered themselves" by betraying others. But they swore that no one had ever been arrested as the result of anything that Hans had confessed.

A few days after Hiller's arrest the SS man Schwarz came to his cell: a comparatively decent fellow, who was in a position of some authority. Schwarz asked him if he would be willing to share a cell with Litten, and keep an eye on him. Litten must not be allowed to commit suicide. Hiller replied that he was willing, though the prospect really dismayed him. The two men were only slightly acquainted, though each knew well enough what opinions the other held. Hiller told Hans exactly what had been required of him, and explained that he would be held responsible if Hans were to take his life while under his charge. The kindly Hans, who would never have allowed another to suffer through any action of his, promised—after some hours of reflection—that he would not lay hands on himself in the cell, so that Hiller could sleep in peace. But he added that wherever Hiller could not be held responsible he would do his very best to end his life.

Hiller, however, was able gradually to dissuade him from taking such a step; reminding him repeatedly how important it was that he should live to continue the fight against National Socialism. Hans, as a matter of fact, felt that he had not now the physical strength or the courage for such an existence, and that even if he should one day recover his liberty he would no longer be a very useful combatant. But he allowed himself to be so far persuaded that he promised to do his best to win through.

Both men were ordered to do the dirtiest and hardest work. They had to scrub the stairs and floors of the prison. No one showed them how to set about such work—and, of course, it was quite strange to them—but behind each worker stood an SS man, who seemed to think that by cursing and kicking them, punching their faces, and striking them with the flat of the sword on buttocks, back and arms they could induce them to do their chores more rapidly and expertly. One such blow wounded Hans in the arm, notching a tendon; he lost much blood, but the wound slowly healed without leaving any lasting disability. Despite the wound, he had to go on working. Since the bandage placed on the wound was stiff with dirt, and was not removed, Hans hoped that some form of blood-poisoning would develop which would send him into hospital or, better still, into the next world.   If the commandant asked him why he was bandaged he had to reply that he had bruised his arm against the door.   This was the reply which every prisoner had to make if questioned as to a wound.

Among the prisoners in this camp were eleven men of Strasser's Black Front.   They were placed in a special division, and were better treated than the rest of the prisoners.   Hans and Kurt Hiller had to do the dirty work of this division.   The men, however, were decent fellows. "We'll do our work ourselves," they told him.   "In the meantime, you take a rest."   They had only to clean the windows, as the cleaners could be seen from outside.

Any former clients of my son's had to strike him "out of gratitude."   They all did it, for if they refused they were brutally manhandled.   Only one of them said: "Strike me dead, but I will not do it!"

Once my son came back from exercise in a state of bewilderment and exhaustion.   He refused to say what had happened.   But here is the report of an eye-witness:

From about the 9th March, 1933, I was imprisoned with about 35 other men in Station VIII of the old Brandenburg jail.   For well over a month I was penned up in a garret, behind a grille.   Trembling at the endless physical and mental brutalities to which we were subjected, we numbered the hours and days of our torment. Whenever one of the two heavy iron doors that gave access to our den even seemed to be moving, there was a shout of "Attention!"   On countless occasions since our arrival we had leapt to our feet as though electrified, standing as though frozen, in accordance with the petti-fogging regulations of the camp. When the doors closed again behind the sentries we collapsed. Between the opening and closing of the doors lay minutes or hours of new torture.

One day an SS troop-leader asked the men in our station: "Who knows Litten?" After a moment's hesitation two of us replied that we did. One was myself; the other a young working-man from Munich. He replied to the question: "How did you come to know him?" with perfect sincerity, betraying his sympathy for Litten, who had defended him successfully in some trifling lawsuit, charging nothing for his services. My acquaintance with Litten was of a general kind. As a student of criminal law I often saw and heard him in the Moabit court.

Barely two hours later a sentry shouted: "The two who knew Litten, come out in the corridor!" With a vague feeling that we had been foolish to admit that we knew him we obeyed the order promptly.... We were marched into the courtyard and in front of the dormitories. There two sentries took charge of us and drove us into the courtyard of the hospital. I don't like to look back on that hour. All that I had suffered up to then faded into insignificance at the sight which met my eyes.

Driven onward by blows and kicks, accompanied by savage abuse, Hans Litten, so befouled and tattered that he was all but unrecognizable, dragged himself across the courtyard. Crawling on his hands and knees, the pitiable victim was compelled to cross the courtyard over and over again.... Two men shouted orders at him in turn. The name of one was Achim Person, a student.

Litten seemed on the point of collapse. Then Person ordered him to hop into the further left-hand corner of the courtyard. Here as everyone knew, was a small pool of liquid filth—a puddle of urine. . . . Holding his head over the puddle, Litten was forced to go down on his hands and knees. To prevent his body from sagging Person took his bayonet and held it point upwards under his victim's abdomen. Then both sentries alternately beat him with the flat of the bayonet on his back and buttocks. This continued until Litten collapsed and fell with his face in the latrine. Bellowed orders and kicks could no longer overcome his apathy. He was dragged out of the courtyard.

The Munich man and I, standing stiffly at attention, had to look on. . . . After Litten had been dragged away the SS men attended to us.

G. Sch.

Kurt Hiller, in the record of his experiences in concentration camps, published in 1935, gave a short description of Hans:

Hans Litten, the learned and valiant defender of Communist prisoners (though he himself was not a member of any political party) and Erich Mühsam are the persons most brutally tortured in this institution. . . . Litten is the most unselfish and helpful of comrades; his kindliness is exceptional; to my thinking he is almost too kindly, for he is good even to scoundrels; a true Christian by nature, and also by conviction; in his involved and baroque ideology Socialistic and Catholic-theocratic motives are blended; he is all for Marx and Lenin, and also for the absolute monarchs of the seventeenth century; he disapproves of the Reformation and the Enlightenment, and of Goethe, but approves of Hölderlin and Rilke; he combines the cult of the proletariat with Mariolatry—and in all this he is perfectly genuine. For a long time we were cell-mates. I shall never forget the *heures bleues* of our philosophical and literary conversations in the prison cell.

After my visit to the commandant things were better in many respects. The heavy work, the punishment drill —and the ordinary exercise was bad enough—were discontinued. The camp was divided into several sections. Two sections were filled with sick, infirm, and aged prisoners. Many others, who enjoyed special protection, found their way into these sections.

On the 1st November, 1933, Hans Litten and Kurt Hiller were transferred to such a section. Hans became more cheerful; he looked better, and even his digestion improved as maltreatment was discontinued. Sometimes he was actually in high spirits. Such success as I had achieved had firmly convinced him that every hour of my life was devoted to him and the betterment of his condition. He seemed to believe that I could work miracles.

When I was receiving such dreadful news of my son's sufferings I called on Frau Sonnemann, the actress, telling her of the commandant's behaviour, and describing the terrible conditions prevailing in the camp. Since I was by no means confident that Conrady would keep his promise, I had asked her in writing for an interview. She rang me up directly she had read my letter, saying that within two hours she was starting on a journey, and would be away for some time. If I would come to her at once she would just have time to see me.

She was already dressed for travelling: a slender, handsome, dignified woman. Despite my anxiety, my first thought was: "How can such a noble-looking woman lower herself by her friendship with Göring!"

She was rather dismayed when I had explained the reason of my call, and described the facts of the case. She had supposed that I wanted to see her in connection with my actor sons, with whom she had some acquaintance. She had been to see her revered teacher, Leopold Jessner, who had told her: "I have a request to make you; I want you to ensure that my pupil Heinz Litten shall be employed again as stage-manager. It would be a pity if the abilities of so gifted a man were wasted; and he has never had anything to do with politics."

She was visibly moved; she even wept, and she cried indignantly: "It is really horrible that such things should keep on happening, although Göring has absolutely forbidden it. Of course, your son must get away from there. I will do everything in my power. Only you mustn't expect that there won't be some delay. To begin with, I am going away for a week. And then I must take advantage of an occasion when I am alone with Göring. And this very rarely happens. The poor man is so terribly overworked. You simply can't imagine how completely he devotes his energies to the welfare of the people. He thinks of nothing else, and his heart bleeds when he has to be hard. And when he is, it is only for the good of the people. And then I must wait for a moment when Göring is in a good temper. If he had just been raging over some Communist I should ruin everything if I were to speak of your son."

I am sure that she really believed what she said—that this was how Göring appeared to her credulous mind. For that matter, it is amazing to note that Göring still contrives to retain a certain popularity among the people. What is still more astonishing is the fact that in foreign countries he is often regarded as the moderate representative of the Nazi régime, and the leader on whom one could place the greatest reliance. Have people forgotten that this man instigated and supervised the burning of the Reichstag, that he was personally responsible for the murder of General Schleicher and his wife, that he has innumerable murders and suicides in the concentration camps on his conscience, and that it is his doing that the headsman's axe is always busy in Germany?

Have they forgotten that his ostentatious wedding with Emmy Sonnemann was signalized by two executions?

CHAPTER VII

An Attempt at Liberation

MARGOT FÜRST had repeatedly declared that we ought to try to arrange for my son's escape, through bribery or other means. It seemed to me, however, that any such attempt would be hopeless. Moreover, I felt that I must never have anything to do with illegal methods. If I were once convicted of anything illegal I should never be allowed to see Hans again.

Margot, knowing what I felt about the matter, had ceased to discuss the possibility of such plans. But I learned, long afterwards, that she had discussed them with a member of an anti-Nazi organization. He had hopes of being able to help her, and he presently sent two SA men to see her; they wore the SA uniform, but were actually Communists who had joined the SA in order to help opposition leaders to escape. Their latest achievement had been the liberation of Scheringer.

For some time past the rumour had been current in Berlin that Scheringer had been abducted by some SA men who had formerly been his supporters, and had been smuggled over the frontier. The confidential agent guaranteed the reliability of the stormtroopers, and Margot gave them all they required of her in order to facilitate the abduction. They asked for money, underclothing, and a suit of my son's, from which an SA uniform was to be made to measure, so that Hans could immediately be put into an SA uniform; it would then be easier for him to travel once he had escaped from the camp.

All the preparations for releasing Hans, and if possible Kurt Hiller, were completed. Unknown to me, the date appointed for the attempt—a few days before Christmas —was approaching. A letter was due from Hans; but it did not arrive. I tried to ring up Margot, and to tell her that no letter had come from Hans; but I could get no reply.

The Fürsts had been arrested a few hours earlier!

Rumour reported that the Fürsts had made an unsuccessful attempt to rescue Hans; that Hans had been shot while trying to escape; that Hans had escaped over the frontier, while the Fürsts were caught.

The only thing which was certain was that my son's letter was overdue. Disquieted by its failure to arrive, and by the rumours which were flying about, I rang up the Gestapo. Dr. Conrady was not accessible, so I questioned a secretary, who replied: "Well, Frau Litten, you must really know why you have had no news!"

"No," I replied, "how should I know? If I had known anything I shouldn't need to ring up the Gestapo."

He: "But you must have heard that the Fürsts were arrested?"

I: "Yes, but I haven't a notion why!"

He: "Oh, well, you'll soon know. You yourself were the object of grave suspicion."

I: "It's the first I've heard of it. May I ask of what I am suspected?"

He: "It doesn't really matter; it was soon obvious that you were innocent."

I: "Well, can I ask why the Fürsts have been arrested? For I positively haven't a notion."

He: "I can give you no information on the subject. But the fact that you have had no news of your son is no doubt connected with their arrest."

As soon as I could get word with Dr. Conrady I asked him why I had no news of my son.

"You can't possibly require of me," he said, "on the top of everything else, that I should see that your son writes to you punctually! No doubt for once he didn't feel inclined to write."

"You know as well as I do," I replied, "that my son would never fail to write the regulation letter. There is something behind the fact that he hasn't written."

I managed to see Conrady again; I told him of the rumours which I had heard concerning Hans, and I took the opportunity of asking him whether the Fürsts' arrest was in any way connected with these rumours. I saw that he was regarding me with suspicion.

"Why do you imagine that their arrest is connected with these rumours?"

"In the first place," I said, "because of the nature of the rumours. In the second place, because you keep on having their apartment searched. I have always taken it for granted that you would be interested in Frau Fürst, because she was my son's secretary, and also because my son was a boarder in her apartment. And I wondered if some sort of an examination was being made, in connection with one of the usual trials."

This seemed to convince him that I really knew nothing definite about the whole affair. He assured me, finally, that I need not be anxious about my son. Hans was quite comfortable, but some sort of an investigation was in progress, and in the meantime he would have to be segregated from the outer world.

And now for weeks I was deprived of all communication with my son. All my requests and efforts were in vain. I was told that I should hear from him again the moment the investigation was concluded. I had no means of knowing whether I was being deceived. I still thought it possible that Hans had been shot while trying to escape, and that the authorities were unwilling to confess the truth. At the same time, I was waiting for news from abroad; for I thought it possible that he had escaped, and I could well imagine that in this also the authorities would be uncommunicative.

In respect of the Fürsts I did nothing whatever; I was

afraid that any activity on my part might be damaging to all of us. Moreover, their parents would look after their interests; they could employ a lawyer, and seek for an explanation of the arrest.

Some three or four months later, when Max Fürst was released, I learned what had happened.

Two Gestapo spies had crept into the organization to which Margot had applied. Apparently it was they who were at the bottom of the plan for abducting Hans; and such arrangements as were made were made by them. For example, the false passport for Hans was prepared by the Gestapo.

When Max Fürst was handed over to the Gestapo he received a few blows on the head—and among his assailants was one of the men who had been consulting with Margot. This told him the truth at once: they had been deluded by spies. Margot, who did not see the SA men after her arrest, denied all knowledge of them in order to protect them!

Max was examined by the Gestapo to the accompaniment of the usual maltreatment. He took all the blame upon himself, in order as far as possible to disculpate his wife. As a reward for his confession he was soundly flogged. When his wife was informed that her husband had made a full confession, so that she had only to explain a few minor points, she exclaimed: "My husband is an idiot! He is simply taking the whole affair on himself in order to save me. He knows nothing whatever about it. That is, he knows what I had in mind, but he was strongly opposed to it. He knows nothing whatever about the details." As she was not believed, she said: "Ask him, then, for certain particulars, and you will see that he knows nothing about them."

This they did. Max lied manfully, but the Gestapo men convinced themselves that he was talking nonsense, and that he really knew nothing. He had been flogged on account of his confession; and he was now flogged because his confession was false. Since they saw that he was practically innocent of the conspiracy he was sent for a few months, by way of a warning, to the Oranienburg camp. There, in the Jewish contingent, he acquired much experience, and he had much to say about the atrocities committed there. While he was interned he was unable to learn what had happened to Margot, and his anxiety was increased by alarming rumours.

While Max was in the Gestapo jail Dr. Conrady deigned to visit him; an unusual distinction.

"What is your profession?" he asked.

"Cabinet-maker."

"Jews don't usually become manual workers. How did you come to be a cabinet-maker?"

"It was just because the Jews are not manual workers," said Max, "that I thought to myself, for once in a way one of them ought to be a cabinet-maker."

"A very good answer," said Conrady, and was gone.

They tried to turn Margot against Hans; she must admit that he was a swine, a man with whom she could have no further dealings. She refused most vehemently to do so, and she made things worse for herself by continually speaking of Hans, and asking for news of him, whenever she saw a visitor, or wrote a letter. She was afraid—and with reason—that she had greatly aggravated his situation by her unsuccessful attempt to liberate him; that he would be further questioned, and brutally maltreated. Every time she saw her mother she asked after me; was I angry with her for getting Hans into worse trouble? I sent her word to the effect that I had nothing to reproach her for; on the contrary, I admired her courage, and her loyalty to Hans.

It is very easy, when an attempt has failed, to say: "How could one be so stupid?" I know much older people, experienced politicians, who have fallen victims to the *agent provocateur*. The very same thing would have happened to me if I had not firmly resolved always to keep within the law.

Margot, unlike so many other women, was never maltreated during her questioning by the Gestapo. She was even treated with a certain respect; and she made quite an impression on the examining magistrate by her courageous and unconcerned bearing. She and her husband exchanged the most delightful and affectionate letters, and the magistrate who censored the correspondence exclaimed one day: "I can't understand how two such accomplished and cultivated people as you and your husband could have thrown yourselves away on such an inferior person as Litten!" This enraged her all the more, in that she felt that whatever intellectual acquirements she might possess, she owed them largely to Hans.

Once, when the *Kriminalkommissar* was questioning her, she was asked how she had come to entertain the crazy idea of attempting to contrive Hans' escape. She replied: "I can understand, of course, that you would wish to prevent such an opponent from working against you. If you had stopped there I should have done nothing. But since you maltreat him so I had to do something to help him." She continued passionately: "You hate him so simply because you are envious, and angry that so fine a man should be fighting against you. You'd be only too glad to have him on your side!" To which the magistrate answered: "Granted. But he doesn't happen to be on our side."

At last the barrister with whom she was allowed a private interview was able to convince her that she would never be released unless she would break off all connection with my son.

She then wrote to her husband, saying that she had realized, during her long imprisonment and separation from her family, that it was her first duty to care for her children. She solemnly promised that she would no longer concern herself with Hans Litten's fate, although her affection and respect for him were unchanged.

She was then released under the Hindenburg amnesty

(which was proclaimed in 1934). I think her release may be attributed to the fact that the gentry of the Gestapo, who had instructed the *agents provocateurs*, had guessed that there was a whole organization at work behind the Fürsts, and were annoyed at having trapped only a temperamental girl.

The Fürsts' business was ruined by this intermezzo. They felt that they were spied upon and threatened at every step. They could do nothing more for Hans; so they left Germany.

.   .   .   .   .

I knew nothing of what had been happening to Hans during these weeks of excitement until I received a full report from Kurt Hiller.

One day—I think it was the 13th December, 1933—all the letters in my son's possession were confiscated, and he was taken, with Kurt Hiller, to the cellar. Only the higher officers of the camp were allowed to approach the cellar; even the prisoners' food was brought by them. This meant that something important was in the wind, concerning which the strictest secrecy was to be observed.

They guessed at once that the change was connected with the plan for their escape, which Margot had explained in code. Hans, as yet, had had no opportunity of replying to her. He could not, while a prisoner in the camp, form any just opinion of the whole plan, and was therefore inclined to distrust it.

Strangely enough, Hans and Kurt Hiller were confined for nearly three days and nights in the same cellar. It was icy cold, and the only light came from without. But they were able to talk things over and decide upon a definite plan. They agreed that Hiller was to know absolutely nothing. Hans was to admit that he knew of the plan, but that he had neither accepted nor rejected it, and he would try to prove, by revealing the code, that he had played an absolutely passive part.

Hiller was examined first, by one of the worst of the Gestapo officials, but in the presence of the commandant, who saw to it that the examination should be objective and conducted in accordance with the legal forms.

The first question was this: Had Litten had any personal contact with an SS man in the Brandenburg camp?

"Yes."

There was a joyful glitter in the eyes of the Gestapo man.

"Describe exactly what happened."

Kurt Hiller told them: an SS man, whose father was involved in a troublesome civil lawsuit, had heard that there was a famous barrister in court. He had asked Litten for his professional advice, which was given. The Gestapo-man's satisfaction was destroyed by the commandant, who explained that these consultations had taken place with his consent and under his supervision, but that apart from them the two men had never met, since they were stationed in different sections of the camp.

Then came the suggestive question: "Did Litten believe at this time that he would be long in the camp, or did he hope to be free very soon?"

"He hoped that he would be set free, as a number of influential people—for example, the Reichswehrminister von Blomberg—were trying to secure his release."

Blomberg's name made a perceptible impression on the commandant.

"What used you to talk about?" was the next question. And Hiller gave a meticulous account of their various discussions of philosophical and literary problems, and of the work of Hölderlin and Rilke. The disillusioned policeman concluded the examination.

After this examination Kurt Hiller was removed to another section. For three weeks longer Hans remained in the cellar, in the strictest solitary confinement.

In the meantime I had persevered in my attempts to help my son, but without result. My petitions were disregarded.

Someone in very close touch with Hindenburg (I have reason to believe that it was Meissner) warned me through a common acquaintance that I should not intercede for my son so vehemently. After all, he had made his bed, and must expect to lie on it. By my intercession I should only bring misfortune on myself and my family.

I was under close observation; I was regarded with the gravest suspicion; it was assumed that I had been implicated in the attempt to enable Hans to escape, but nothing had been proved against me.

I sent him my thanks for his friendly counsel, but I told him that I was surprised that he should seriously give me the unethical advice to abandon my son to his fate. If I should bring misfortune upon my family by trying to assist him—well, that couldn't be helped; and both my other sons had declared that I was not to think of them for a moment; they took it as a matter of course that their brother's fate must be the first consideration.

But misfortune did not overlook them.

CHAPTER VIII

The Fate of the Younger Sons

My youngest son, Rainer, had dissolved his contract with the Leipzig theatre in order to work in Berlin. In Alsberg's *Konflikt* he was to play an important part in conjunction with Bassermann and Frau Durieux. He wanted to choose a theatrical pseudonym, as the Nazi Press was constantly attacking his brother. But the director of the theatre would not agree to this; the cast of this play included only "prominent" artists, and he was thankful to have found for this definitely juvenile part a young actor who had proved his mettle and whose name was not wholly unknown.

On the day when the opening performance of *Konflikt* was first advertised in detail, the *Vossische Zeitung* contained the three following announcements:

"The barrister, Hans Litten, was taken into protective custody on the night of the Reichstag fire.

"The stage manager of the Chemnitz theatre, Dr. Heinz Litten, has been dismissed without notice.

"Rainer Litten is to play the part of Christoph in *Konflikt*."

The director regretted that he had not allowed Rainer to change his name; but now it was too late.

After playing in *Konflikt* my son took the part of Peter in *Flüchtlingen*, the first "national film" made by Ufa. Once more Rainer wanted to change his name; again his request was refused, for the same reason.

Before the film had been released to the public Rainer was already working with Albers on another film. He was beginning to attract attention; he was regarded as a rapidly rising young star; and the Nazi Press was constantly singing his praises. He was "what the German soul dreamed itself to be"; he was "*the* German youth." The critics fought for the honour of having discovered him.

But then one of his interviewers learned of his relation to Hans Litten, and reported his discovery to Ufa. It was all up with his career. He could not be cut out of the *Flüchtlingen* film, but there was just time to alter the proscribed name before the first showing. From the second film there was still time to banish him in person. He claimed the payment of his salary in court, and won his case. (He was clever enough to choose a Nazi officer, a *Standartenführer*, to represent him.) The magistrate who made the award was removed from the Bench.

Rainer was given a part in a privately-owned theatre, with the comment: "No one can interfere with us here." But on the night of the opening performance SA men stood in front of the theatre, challenging the playgoers, as they arrived, "in the name of the Party," to boycott the piece. When they asked "Why?" they replied: "On account of the barrister Litten's brother."

Nevertheless, the theatre was sold out; but on the third day the director told Rainer that he could not allow him to appear again; the Nazis had threatened to close the theatre if Rainer Litten appeared on the stage. But he would take it as a favour if Rainer would sue him for his salary. He would naturally win his suit, and the director could claim the amount from the Party.

But Rainer's advocate explained: "I dare not represent you again, and I advise you, if you want to keep a whole bone in your body, to clear out of Germany with all possible speed."

Which Rainer did.

.   .   .   .   .

My second son, Heinz, had fled from Chemnitz by night, driving to Berlin through the darkness and the mist, and was now living with us. For the first few weeks he had slept each night in the house of a different friend, but in Berlin he was apparently to be left in peace. In Chemnitz the Nazis had searched for him dog-whip in hand; they had posted a guard at the railway station, in order to arrest him if he should try to leave the town. He was no politician; he belonged to no party; but he had been guilty of a great imprudence.

An actor with whom he was on terms of intimate friendship, one Karl Heinz Stein, of whom the manager had no great opinion, had reason to fear that he would not be engaged for the next season. "Very well," he said, "I shall insure myself."

The manager had already given notice, on artistic grounds, to a member of the Nazi Party, whereupon the Party informed him that unless he recalled his notice they would fight him tooth and nail. He could not, for the sake of his reputation, recall his notice on account of such a threat, but he knew very well that in Chemnitz, where the Nazis had the upper hand, he would never again dare to dismiss a Nazi if he wanted to retain his position.

The result was that all those actors who did not feel certain of employment poured into the ranks of the Party. Stein even became an SA man, and was soon playing an important part in local politics. When Heinz heard of this, he told him: "You're a swine, and I'll have nothing more to do with you."

From this day onwards his productions were violently attacked by the National Socialist organs, and by other journals in sympathy with the Party, though hitherto they had been praised in terms of absolute enthusiasm by critics of all parties.

He was guilty, too, of another mistake. He produced plays with pacifistic and socialistic motives, and he rehearsed the SAJ (Socialistische Arbeiter Jugend) in spoken choruses for their fêtes.

After the coup d'état the turncoat Stein became manager, and the first thing he did was to dismiss, without notice, every member of the company who did not enjoy his favour, beginning with the then manager. This was a magnificent opportunity for taking his revenge for all former personal differences.

The new manager had a placard posted outside the theatre: "Dr. Heinz Litten is forbidden to enter the theatre." From the balcony of the theatre the storm-trooper and critic of the Nazi newspaper, *Ballerstedt*, in a state of imbecile intoxication, informed the roaring crowd that the brother of Hans Litten, "the defender of Red murderers," must be "prevented from doing further harm." The same gentleman amused himself by forcing his way into houses in order to conduct searches and make arrests. The person who opened the door, whether man or woman, was promptly greeted by a blow on the face or a kick.

The editor of the *Volksstime*, an old, invalidish man, was shot "in self-defence" by stormtroopers who were making a perquisition in his office. Needless to say, he was shot in the back, like so many of those who were killed "in self-defence."

After this Heinz felt that it would be inexpedient to remain any longer in Chemnitz.

He, too, had claimed the payment of salary due to him. Unfortunately, he chose no *Standartenführer*, no troop-leader to represent him, but a simple advocate. But seeing that the defendant, Manager Stein, appeared before the court in the full uniform of a troop-leader, to be faced by an ordinary advocate, wearing no party insignia, it is needless to record the decision of the court. The witnesses "had no recollection of the matter," and the chief witness found that he was too unwell to give evidence. Another had honestly written to Hans; would he please not put him in the unpleasant position of having to give evidence against his present employer? If he did give his evidence he would lose his position, which he had reached after such a struggle, etc.

Heinz lost his case. The magistrate, who gave his decision with obvious discomfort, had proposed a settlement out of court. But Karl Heinz Stein was adamant. "By no means!" he exclaimed. "After such a settlement Litten would be able to find employment again. That I mean to prevent under any circumstances."

He has prevented it.

Heinz could not as yet make up his mind to leave Germany. He felt that someone ought to remain and help me in my fight for Hans. He gave dramatic tuition to various Berlin actors, including even some from the State theatre.

CHAPTER IX

In Hospital

AT LAST, on the 1st February, 1934, I heard from Hans that he had been removed to Esterwegen. One paragraph of his letter made me uneasy.

"The work here on the moor is terribly strenuous; but now that I have been here ten days I have the impression that I can do it as far as my muscles are concerned. But, of course, I don't know how long my heart will hold out. (Please send me again in the next package my medicine for cardiac spasms.) It is some consolation to me that I can approve of the purpose of the task (cultivating moorland), and above all things, the landscape is wonderful: a very wide plain, almost without a tree, an unlimited prospect in all directions. Most people find this depressing, but you know how I love just such a plain.—It reminds me strongly of our East Prussian plains.—Of course, I can't manage any intellectual work; I am much too tired for that. At most I read a few lines of Hölderlin or Shakespeare in the evening."

I asked Dr. Conrady at once for a visitor's permit. He apparently thought my intention of going to Esterwegen highly ridiculous, and he was not at all inclined to give me a permit, as visitors, it seemed, were not usually admitted at this camp. However, I reminded him of his promise: "Directly the examination is concluded you can get into touch with your son again." So at last I received the permit.

I reached Papenburg in the evening, just before the office was closed. The official whom I saw at the *Kommandantur*—apparently a police officer—was quite charming in his manner to me: he explained that I should have to make a long journey by motor-car, but that he would engage the car himself, as it would then be cheaper, and he would accompany me. I replied that no doubt his time was valuable; I could very well go alone; but he would not be dissuaded. He also advised me, in quite a paternal manner, about lodgings; I must be sure to get a room with a stove, as the climate there was cold and foggy. In short, he was most friendly and agreeable.

When I called for him on the following day he had already rung up the camp, and had learned that my son had met with a slight mishap. This, however, was all to the good, as he would not have to be brought in from his work, and I could speak to him at once.

During the whole journey we conversed in the most friendly manner. I wondered whether the people at the camp would admit my big package of food; he promised me that he would see to the matter. At last we came to an endless barbed-wire fence; a dismal sight. I could see no prisoners at work anywhere.

When we reached the camp, the entrance to which was heavily guarded, I was questioned as to the contents of my package. My companion took it from me, saying: "It's all right, I've inspected it already."

Hans was in a sick-ward; the only occupant. He looked feverish. He told me: "I have very often fainted lately, on account of these cardiac spasms. I had one when I was driving on a lorry. What happened then I don't know. I only know that when I came to my senses again there had been an accident to my leg; the wheel of a lorry had gone over it."

I asked him whether he could not ask to be excused from heavy work, owing to the state of his heart. He replied: "No, I am sure that would be quite useless."

At this moment a young doctor came into the ward. Hans immediately lay stiff as a ramrod, and during the whole of the doctor's visit he held his arm outstretched above the bed in a "Heil Hitler" salute.

The doctor threw back the bedclothes. I saw that one leg was tightly bandaged. The doctor asked him roughly: "How are things to-day?"

"I'm in frightful pain," said Hans.

"Then I expect you'll have to go into hospital; it's probably a fracture."

For five days Hans had been lying there, in ghastly pain, and in a high fever, before the doctor could make up his mind.

"May I take this opportunity," I said, "of calling your

attention to the fact that my son suffers from a heart complaint which has been greatly aggravated during his imprisonment? He cannot possibly do heavy physical work in this condition. His accident shows how serious the results of doing such work can be."

The doctor shouted at me: "What do you mean? Of course he can work!" and disappeared. Hans looked at me as much as to say: "Do you understand now why I don't report myself as sick?"

The official who had accompanied me was present during the interview. There was no one else in the ward. He now picked up the package. "I must just look into this; after all, I can't pass it absolutely without inspection." He seemed so absorbed in his examination of its contents that I felt that he would pay no further attention to our conversation.

Hans cautiously pressed a finger to his lips and gave me a warning glance. I began, very cautiously, to question him; and as he did not answer me frankly I asked him the question outright: "I want to know whether you are ill-treated here." Hans replied that apart from the "greeting" on his arrival nothing had happened. There was no way of telling whether this was the truth.

The official gave Hans the package and informed me that it was time for me to go. He had allowed us to talk for more than an hour.

I had some scruples of conscience in respect of my question as to ill-treatment, although the official had not protested in any way. So during the drive back to Papenburg I referred to the matter. "I must ask you to forgive me," I said, "for questioning my son as to whether he had been maltreated. But you will understand when I tell you that he has over and over again been terribly maltreated."

My companion received this as though it was the first time he had even heard of such a thing. He simply could not believe it. Here at all events nothing of the kind ever happened. That was quite out of the question. The prisoners were extremely comfortable here. When I suggested that he really could not be sure of that, since he did not live in the camp, he told me the touching story of a well-known professor who had been sent to the camp. His family had done everything possible to get him out, as he had been offered a good position abroad. But he was so comfortable in the camp that he refused to leave it.

Afterwards I questioned some of this professor's friends, to learn that he had made every possible effort to get away from Esterwegen; and he declared that the most terrible things had happened there.

We continued to converse in the most amiable fashion, and I was careful not to betray my suspicion that this man might have had orders from the Gestapo to see what amiability would do to lead me to confide in him.

As we drove past it he pointed to the Marien-Hospital, to which my son would be sent. Once Hans was there, he thought, he would remain there for some time, as the roads were so bad for traffic.

I got back to Papenburg just in time to catch the last train that evening. The journey was tedious, with many changes. Almost as soon as the train had started I began to reproach myself for not having got into touch with the staff of the hospital. Ought I to get out at the next station? But it was important that I should get back to Berlin as quickly as possible; then I could make inquiries about the doctor and the hospital, and if need be make another scene at the Gestapo.

Two days later I received a letter from Hans. On the very day of my visit he had been transferred to the hospital.

"According to the X-ray photograph the leg is not broken; there is only a greenstick fracture of the fibula, and also a severe extravasation of blood in the kneejoint. The leg is just as painful as ever, so that I cannot write as fully as I should like. Please send me no packages at present; the food here is excellent and abundant, much better than I was able to afford for the last few years before my arrest."

Then I heard no more from him.

I learnt by inquiry that the director of the hospital had formerly been an army surgeon, and that he was well spoken of in medical circles, so that Hans, in so far as this was possible in so small a hospital, would receive careful and skilful treatment.

I wrote to the doctor, enclosing a letter from a specialist which certified that Hans was suffering from a form of heart disease. I begged him to treat my son for this trouble while he was in the hospital, and to make sure that after his discharge he was not put to labour unsuitable for one in his state of health. I received no answer. Hans told me afterwards, in a letter, that the doctor wished me to know that he had examined the heart and had found that it "wasn't so bad."

Since after my first news of Hans I heard no more I applied to the Kommandantur. Again there was no reply, so I wrote to the hospital. I received a brief official intimation that in such matters I must apply to the Kommandantur. The hospital could give no information in respect of persons in protective custody. But a tiny note had been slipped into the envelope:

> Destroy at once and tell no one. Your son is in the best of hands here with us. We are doing all that is in our power to make things easier for him. SISTER ——.

She had signed her name!

As I still had no news of Hans, I became so uneasy, despite this note, that I spoke of nothing else. "Just ring up the hospital," said Heinz, "ring them up about noon, as though it were a matter of course, and ask how the Rechtsanwalt Litten is going on; as though your son were not a prisoner but an ordinary patient. If you catch them off their guard they may tell you."

It happened just as he foretold. The sister who had sent me the comforting note was called to the telephone; and she gave me a clear and exhaustive account of my son's condition. He was in a high fever, and the contused wound was suppurating freely, but he was no longer actually in danger. He was being treated with applications of peat and diathermy.

When I asked her why I could get absolutely no direct news of him I could hear, through the telephone, that something had startled her; and then she said, in a loud, sharp tone: "No, I absolutely cannot give you any information whatever. You must simply apply to the Kommandantur."

Gradually the exchange of letters began again. My son's condition was still far from satisfactory; but "as for the rest," he said, "the treatment and the nursing are splendid." This sentence was underlined with a blue pencil—apparently by the censor.

On the 13th May, 1934—that is, after nearly three months in hospital—Hans was sent back to Esterwegen as a convalescent. He wrote that he was well again but for an absolutely stiff knee. The doctor had told him that this knee required long and very careful treatment— radiation, massage, exercise with special apparatus, etc.— before he could bend it again; but, of course, there was no possibility of that in camp.

CHAPTER X

The Bar under the Terror

HANS HAD ASKED ME in his first letter from Esterwegen to inquire of Dr. Conrady whether criminal proceedings were pending against him. The commissar who had examined him in Brandenburg had said that if no such proceedings were pending he could engage an advocate who would be allowed to represent him. He therefore enclosed a signed power of attorney for the advocate, and also a record of his former activities. Of this I reproduce the more important passages:

I was taken into protective custody on the 28th February, 1933. No concrete grounds for this measure have ever been given me! Apparently it was grounded in a very general fashion on my former activity as counsel for the defence in a large number of Communist trials. As a consequence of this activity—in which the Ministry of Justice sees evidence of Communism in the sense of the statute relating to advocates—my admission to the bar was cancelled in July 1933.

No criminal proceedings are pending against me. The reasons for my prolonged detention are unknown to me.

In many cases known to me even officials of the KPD (Communist Party) have been released after a much briefer turn. Nevertheless, I should like to adduce a few points which may possibly be of significance in any application for release:

From the remonstrances which have repeatedly been addressed to me during my detention it would seem that many people believe that I played a prominent part in the KPD.

This is not so. I have never at any time been a member of the KPD, and this not only for formal reasons, but on account of important political differences. Since 1925 I have fought against the Parliamentary and industrial policy of the KPD, against their optimistic valuation of Russia, and against their dependence on the Moscow Central (which I regarded as an instrument of Russian foreign policy). I have always, when necessary, laid emphasis on this attitude, even in court. Also, when I have referred in public meetings of the *Rote Hilfe* to any sort of legal proceedings, I have dissociated myself from the KPD. In consequence of this attitude I have never appeared for the defence in any lawsuit in which anything was at stake for the KPD *as such*. This, for example, explains why in spite of my great success as counsel for the defence I have never appeared for the defence against a charge of high treason in the Supreme Court. On the other hand, I have often appeared in court, as the representative of oppositional Communist or Anarchist groups against the KPD; in particular, before the Lichtenberg police-court in proceedings against the former city councillors and district guardians (*Bezirksversteher*). I am quite aware that my former political attitude cannot be much more sympathetic to the National Government than that of the KPD, but I think it is useful to explain this attitude, as the erroneous notion which seems to obtain of my alleged role in the KPD may possibly be to some extent responsible for the duration of my detention.

. . . I have often had to contend with the belief that when I have appeared in court against the SA I have attacked them with special hostility. As a matter of fact, I suppose no Communist advocate has been so just to political opponents in court. When I have represented persons claiming damages for injuries inflicted by SA men I have always acted on the principle, in reviewing the evidence, that I would ask for no sentence for which I would not be responsible were I the judge. For this reason, as joint plaintiff I have often moved for an acquittal. In one case (Foyer and others) I moved for no sentence against the principal accused, although the Public Prosecutor had moved for a sentence of ten years' imprisonment, because it seemed to me that the objection that he had been hopelessly intoxicated had not been rebutted. In all these cases I have vehemently insisted on the *personal honesty* of the political opponent and on the acceptance of the view that he acted in obedience to his convictions. In one case (Stief and others) I even applied—unsuccessfully—for a new trial, on the grounds that the assize court had unjustly found that the prisoner had not acted out of conviction. All this is recorded in the archives.

I do not wish to lay special emphasis on my attitude in

such matters, which is, I think, a matter of course in a decent human being; but I am obliged to insist on this correction in view of the constant assertions to the contrary.

Hans gave me the name of an advocate who had been able to secure the release of a number of persons in protective custody.

I explained the situation to Dr. Conrady, and he replied: "Don't you put yourself to the trouble; your son can't entrust his case to any advocate. It's true that no criminal proceedings are pending against him, but he won't be allowed to employ an advocate!" I said that I should appeal to a higher authority; then, perhaps, I should obtain the required permission. But he laughed scornfully, saying: "Even if you get permission there isn't an advocate in Germany who would act for your son!"

Dittrich, the advocate whom my son had named, was evidently flattered to think that his reputation had justified his selection. I saw at once that he was a man of little ability, who owed his position to his party membership. After I had been talking to him for some five minutes, during which he had observed me with peculiar interest, he said: "Excuse the interruption, but aren't you then a Jewess? No, you can't have any Jewish blood in you! That's out of the question!"

"I have already told you," I said, "that I am not a Jewess."

"But how is that possible?"

"You say that, I suppose, because Herr Goebbels is always speaking of the Jew Litten? Herr Goebbels is doubtless powerful enough to stifle any refutation of his statements, but his power doesn't extend so far that he can alter the blood in my veins!"

Dittrich became more obliging in his manner. He would be delighted to help me, but he must first ask the Party whether it would allow him to undertake the case.

Of course, his final reply (six weeks later) was that to his great regret it would be impossible for him to undertake the case; the Party had forbidden it.

When Dr. Conrady asked me, rather scornfully, some time later, whether I had found an advocate, I replied: "I gave up trying after my first attempt. It appears to need courage. And no German has any courage nowadays."

"How can you say such a thing!" he exclaimed.

"That is not a mere assertion," I said, "it's an indisputable fact that everyone in the Third Reich is trembling with fear!"

Of course, I did look about me for other advocates. One, who was very fond of Hans, and who, since he was well on the Right in politics, was not in any danger, was willing to risk a rebuff. He received it. Litten, he was informed, would not be allowed a legal representative.

Others, who as far as outward appearances went were on good terms with the Third Reich, told me at once that no advocate either could or would be allowed to help my son. They offered to advise me at a secret consultation, but no one must hear of the interview, and I must never speak my name over the telephone. I had even to give a false name to the office staff. None of these men would accept any fee from me.

One of them told me that it was of the utmost importance that I should get into touch with people in England; and generally, to interest eminent foreigners in my son's case.

When Conrady was replaced by Tessmer, and the latter obstinately refused to see me, my advocate, who was personally acquainted with many of these State attorneys, suggested an explanation: "It is simply that he knows that it's dangerous to have anything to do with you. You have already done for two of them!" As I vehemently denied that I had done anyone—even Conrady—any harm whatever, he replied: "But you were always having interviews with him, though he wouldn't see anyone else; do you think that didn't damage him? Or the fact that he repeatedly told his friends that you were 'his favourite client.'"

When I called on this advocate some time later he stared at me in dismay. "Go away at once!" he cried. "I am just starting on a journey. They told me to-day at the Gestapo that they were quite aware that I was interested in the Litten case, and they asked me whether perhaps I wanted to be treated as Sack was treated!" (Sack was sent to a concentration camp after 30th June, not because he had defended Torgler, but on account of his friendship with the group-leader Ernst, who was murdered on the 30th June.)

Another advocate advised me to apply to a Mr. Cape. This was all very strange and mysterious. I was not to mention the name of my advisers, but Mr. Cape, on the other hand, was most anxious to learn who had sent me to him. I did not learn where he himself was living; I met him in a hotel, to which his letters were directed. He promised to speak to Göring, but he did not think he could give me much hope. The cases in which he had been able to help people had been much less difficult.

Not until long afterwards did my advocate enlighten me as to the identity of this mysterious Mr. Cape. He was an American financier who was transferring huge sums of money to foreign countries for Göring—and probably for other Nazi bonzes. After each transference of capital he begged for the release of an internee. So Mr. Cape was in the service of the Nazis and of their opponents.

I had a rather different experience with an Austrian advocate, Dr. Braun-Stammfest, Wien I, Graben 14.

Friends in Vienna had written to tell me that Dr. Braun-Stammfest had offered to obtain my son's release. They did not like him, but they knew that he had already got a number of people out of the concentration camps. He was coming to Berlin very shortly, and I ought at least to get into touch with him.

Of course, I did so. He himself did not come to see me; he was too busy; but he sent his brother. He explained that the situation was as follows: Dr. Braun-Stammfest was an influential Austrian Nazi; Hitler would therefore be particularly amiable to him, and would hardly refuse a request of his. He had already on the previous day had an interview with Hitler, at which he presented the Führer, in the name of the Austrian Nazis, with a valuable grandfather's clock, which had once, in Vienna, been in the possession of Napoleon. (Of course, the exportation of such an object was illegal, but that did not matter to a Nazi.) Hitler had been greatly pleased by this proof of loyalty, and had been most gracious; and Dr. Braun-Stammfest had taken the opportunity of telling Hitler that he was interested in the release of Hans Litten. Hitler had given him a friendly clap on the shoulder, saying: "We'll talk of that matter again some time; no doubt I shall be able to do you this service." Of course, my visitor explained, the matter would take a little time; but it was really as good as settled; and of course it would cost a little money—about six thousand marks—and a deposit of a thousand marks.

We gave this gentleman as much as we had in the house as a preliminary payment. He would call for the rest on the first opportunity; he was always coming to Germany on business.

Before long we received a letter. The matter presented no difficulties; everything was being arranged through a highly placed personage in Vienna. (The allusion could only be to von Papen.) I must first of all ask my son to promise that he would pledge himself never again to act as advocate, and to refrain from any sort of political activity.

I replied that he apparently was not taking the matter seriously enough; for otherwise he must have learned that my son had long ago been struck off the roll of advocates, and that in any case I should not be allowed to discuss such matters with him. He must negotiate with my son directly, through the Gestapo.

Soon after this a certain Herr Dehnhard came to see me (a parachutist!), whom Dr. Braun-Stammfest had previously introduced as his representative. He took the rest of the advance payment, and assured me that all was going well, but the matter would have to be negotiated through another channel. A neurologist who held a high position in the Nazi Party would examine Hans as to the state of his nerves; he would certify that he was unfit for detention, would receive him into his sanatorium, and would keep him under treatment until his actual release was secured. This method was more agreeable to the responsible Government officials.

Soon after this, as I was spending a few weeks in Switzerland, I wrote to Dr. Braun-Stammfest that we could now discuss the matter in writing without let or hindrance. Despite several reminders, he did not reply, but he told the Viennese friend who had recommended him that things were going well. Nothing more could ever be elicited from him; things were going well!

Dr. Braun-Stammfest had really been very successful in obtaining the release of prisoners; but it turned out that these were Nazis, who had been interned in the Wöllersdorf camp!

PART II
LICHTENBERG

Fighting for a Permit

I first heard of the existence of the Lichtenberg camp on the 7th June, 1934. Hans had suddenly been taken there. On inquiry I learned that it was a comparatively tolerable camp, mainly for the reception of ailing and invalid prisoners.

A request for a visitor's permit was rudely refused.

A letter from Hans, in which he asked for a new pair of spectacles, worried me greatly. Very often, when he had been maltreated, his glasses had been broken, so that I imagined that he was really telling me that he had been maltreated again. He also wrote that he was often reminded of the "Annunciation" in Bamberg Cathedral. This Annunciation differs from other representations of the subject; the angel is not bringing "tidings of great joy," but is pressing his hand upon Mary's forehead, as though laying all the woes of the world upon her head.

I felt perfectly certain that this was meant to convey something, and I urgently begged Conrady to grant me an interview. He was not yet back from leave. This was shortly after 20th June, 1934. Both Conrady and Deils had been removed from their posts, and Himmler was now the leader of the Gestapo.

Dr. Tessmer, Conrady's successor, refused over the telephone to give me an interview. Visitors' permits were not given except in cases of urgent economic necessity. My son was going on well. I told him that I was anxious on account of the state of my son's health and the still unhealed leg. He replied: "You can feel convinced that in the camp he will be treated with the usual consideration," to which I retorted: "Yes, with the consideration that has made him a cripple!" Tessmer blazed up at this. "How dare you say such a thing over the telephone!" My reply to that was: "How else am I to say it if you won't see me?" But that, unfortunately, got me no further.

Once, however, I did succeed in obtaining an interview with Tessmer; it was when I had a complaint to make. He did not discuss the complaint, but pressed me urgently to tell him where I got my information. I replied: "Dr. Tessmer, you don't know me yet. I know that your time is very valuable, and that on this account you have always refused to see me. In order to save you from wasting your valuable time on useless questions I had better solemnly inform you that I would sooner be hacked into little pieces while still alive than betray people who have helped me. Now I have said this do you want to ask me any more questions?" He coloured up and said, quietly and positively, "No!" But he never gave me an interview again.

I now wrote to Herr von Blomberg, although I had really determined, after his recent behaviour, that I would not apply to him again. I took the letter to the Ministry, hoping that I might be able to speak to him, but the doorkeeper informed me that Herr von Blomberg was on holiday in Sweden. This doorkeeper was a rather talkative man, still full of the events of the 30th June, and the exciting and dangerous situation in which the whole Reichswehr Ministry had found itself. And since I listened to all with an expression of admiring interest, we were soon such good friends that he promised me that my letter should not go through the office, but that he would smuggle it into the mail which would be sent off to Herr von Blomberg. A few days later I had a reply from his adjutant, a rather smudgy picture-postcard from Helsingfors.

> Most honoured and gracious lady, your lines reached the R.W.M. here on a foreign tour. About the middle of August he will be back in Berlin. Kindly ring up again then. Heil Hitler, Yours, v. A——.

This sounded as though Blomberg's attitude was more hopeful than I had thought.

My husband, who at my express wish had hitherto remained abroad, now returned, as the transfer and exchange of currency were becoming more difficult. Nothing had happened to me, and I did not think he would now be in personal danger. However, he kept very much in the background; if only for my son's sake, we could not risk the loss of his pension.

I often discussed with my husband the best way of approaching Blomberg. "If only I could have a talk with him!" said my husband. "I could soon persuade him to be reasonable. We have always been on such excellent terms, and he has so often asked my advice in confidential affairs, that he would surely be ready to help me!"

"Well, then," I said, "go to see him. I quite agree with what you say, and you can't be running any risk in going to see your old friend Blomberg."

Blomberg returned sooner than was expected, owing to the death of Hindenburg. My husband wrote to him. The adjutant replied:

The Reichswehr Minister's time is so fully occupied owing to the death of the General Field-Marshal and the subsequent events that he cannot receive callers. If you will explain your business to me I shall be very pleased to see you here, on the condition that your business is not of a political nature.

"Under these circumstances," my husband exclaimed, "I can't possibly go to see him; it would evidently be quite useless, and as a retired captain I can't allow myself to be thrown out with the comment that I came under false pretences." He wrote to the adjutant saying that under the circumstances he would not ask for an interview.

On the following day I rang up the adjutant. "I have just heard," I said, "that my husband has written to you. He has told me that he cannot, as an ex-captain, run the risk of being thrown out of your office. But in my opinion the matter in question is not political. I am going to ask you to see me in his place. You can turn me out with equanimity if you like. My honour will not be injured. I should simply conclude that we had different opinions as to what are and what are not 'political matters.' "

"Didn't you get my card from Sweden?" he asked. "Of course I am willing to see you. You have only to come at once."

He was sitting at his desk, looking very slender and elegant in his white uniform. He was holding a riding-whip in his hand, which he waved in a light, graceful gesture that seemed to indicate that he did not want to delve too deeply into things. However, this did not prevent me from speaking my mind. He listened attentively, and then made the usual comment: "You know, of course, that Herr von Blomberg, with the best will in the world, is simply not in a position to do anything. You know the law, I suppose, that no department can meddle in the affairs of another?"

"Oh," I said, "if Herr von Blomberg really wanted to do anything he could do it, all the same!"

"But what do you imagine he could do?" asked the adjutant. "We are absolutely unpolitical, and we are not allowed to implicate ourselves in political affairs. Thank God, we have no concern with politics! We stand behind our Führer, and that is all that concerns us."

"If I were Herr von Blomberg," I said, "I should pound my fist on the table at the next Cabinet meeting and say: 'I, Herr von Blomberg, have a good name to lose. I am a member of the Cabinet. People think abroad that this enables me to exert a certain amount of influence, and they will hold me equally responsible with you for the unheard-of abominations which are constantly being committed in this country. I go no further with you unless you see to it that these things are stopped.'"

The adjutant smiled. "Yes, gracious lady, that is what you would do. Of that I am perfectly confident. But Herr von Blomberg will never do anything like that."

"Well, then," I said, "if I am doing no good here, do at least advise me as to what I can do!"

"Apply direct to Himmler," he said. "Write to him and ask for an interview. But write to him amiably, and be very polite. Say nothing about swinish abominations and crimes or he will never see you. If you can once obtain an interview, you can express yourself as vehemently as you have done to me. Perhaps you will make some impression on him."

So I wrote very amiably and politely to Himmler, referring to an injunction issued by Hess, and published in the *Volkische Beobachter* of the 24th January, 1934; and in particular to the following passage: "Whosoever in justified concern for the movement, giving his name requests my intervention in respect of obnoxious persons and corruptors of morals among the leaders of the NSDAP, can always look to me for protection." I added that I had a matter of importance to lay before him, and that it was in the interest of the State to give me a hearing.

As soon as my letter was delivered Himmler's personal adjutant rang me up to tell me that Himmler was out of town for the moment, but that he, the adjutant, could see me.

At the Gestapo I was received by Captain A.; his manners were good, and he was perfectly courteous. I told him that I should have to say all sorts of things that he would not find at all pleasing. I was afraid I might make a bad impression on him. Perhaps he would care to make inquiries; in that case I would refer him to Herr von Blomberg, who knew me very well.—I hoped, by saying this, to ensure a respectful hearing.—I continued by saying that I knew that Himmler was the person to whom I should bring such complaints as I had to make. Could I speak to him, the adjutant, as I could to Himmler, according to Hess's injunction?

He assured me that I should not suffer for anything that I might have to say. And he, as Himmler's adjutant, was as competent as Himmler to receive my statement.

I therefore let myself go, describing, from the very beginning, all the abominable things that had been done; and I explained that I was now more anxious than ever; in the first place, because I had been refused a visitor's permit; in the second place, because my son had asked for a new pair of spectacles, which meant, I suppose, that his glasses had been smashed again; and in the third place, because an English lady who had recently called on me had asked me for news of my son's health. His English colleagues had not heard from him since his accident, and there were rumours that he had lost a leg through the accident, and also that he was dead.

He tried to reassure me. I ought not to pay any attention to such foolish rumours; after all, any news that came from the Communists were a pack of lies.

"You must forgive me," I said, "if I am of a different opinion. I am no Communist; but whatever I have heard from Communist sources hitherto has turned out to be the truth; while it's a fact that the gentlemen of the Gestapo have lied to me through thick and thin."

He then said the usual things about a mother's nervousness. But I could really be quite easy now, for even if such things had actually happened they had been cases of wholly unprecedented abuses of power, and now that Herr Himmler had matters in hand they would be most severely punished. "If we ever discover such things we shall go for them hammer and tongs."

I replied that this, unfortunately, did not reassure me,

for immediately after the advent of Herr Himmler one of the Gestapo's most horrible crimes had been committed: the murder of Mühsam. It was just this that worried me so, for I had heard it rumoured that Mühsam's murderer had cried: "Well, *he's* done for! now it's the turn of that swine Litten!"

I was of course reproved for believing such nonsense. Besides, I must have read in the newspapers that Mühsam had hanged himself. I told him that I placed much more reliance on my information than on the reports in the Press, and that I had learned from a reliable source that Mühsam was murdered. I had been given a full description of the whole incident; moreover, all those who knew anything of Mühsam knew that on political grounds he was absolutely opposed to suicide. But actually the point was not important. If after eighteen months of the most brutal maltreatment this man had really been driven to suicide, this spoke almost more forcibly against the conditions in the camps than his murder would have done.

The adjutant tried to persuade me that it was perfectly comprehensible that a man of Mühsam's age might have said to himself, in the silence of the night: "You'll never get out of here again." However well he was treated, such a thought might lead him to make an end.—But at last, when he saw that I stuck to my own point of view, he said: "I'll relieve you of that anxiety; you shall convince yourself personally whether the leg has been saved."

He rang up Tessmer in my presence. Tessmer, of course, was the very man who had refused me a visitor's permit. From a long conversation over the telephone I gathered that Tessmer was vehemently protesting against the issue of a permit, and that finally Himmler's adjutant practically ordered him to give me one. Before I left, Captain H. declared once more that every Communist was a rascal; that he had had personal experience of them; to which I replied that he had been unfortunate. A great many students used to visit our house, and almost always, if one of them seemed so attractive that I received him as a friend of the family, he confided to me the fact that he was a Communist.

I then went, as I was directed, to Herr Tessmer, in order to obtain my permit. Tessmer, however, refused to see me. He was apparently furious that I had succeeded in getting my way in spite of him.

The secretary who had to make out the permit informed me: "You must give me an economic reason for the visit; that is a condition of the permit." I exclaimed, now thoroughly irritated by this new obstacle, that I had no economic reasons for wishing to see my son. To this the secretary replied, amiably: "Don't distress yourself. We must think up a reason." At last a genuine reason occurred to me: among the documents belonging to one of my son's clients, which were of course confiscated, were a few valuable bills; he wanted to secure their return, and had written to me on the subject. The secretary thought this would count as an economic reason, and the matter could be more readily cleared up if I were to discuss it with my son.

Catholic friends had recommended me to a Catholic priest in Berlin who was engaged in welfare work among the prisoners, and was doing his very utmost to ameliorate the lot of the victims of the Nazi Government. He already knew the facts of my son's case. He beamed with delight when I described my various encounters with the Gestapo; such fanatics for the truth, he said, were invaluable in the campaign against the Nazis. I told him that I needed the help of a courageous clergyman who would visit my son in order to bring me news of him. Perhaps he could visit him on the pretext of hearing his confession. My son, it was true, had been baptized a Protestant, but he always had a leaning toward the Catholic faith. (His friendship with Father Stratmann obviously made a good impression on the priest.) I was appealing now to a Catholic because I knew of many cases in which the Catholic clergy had been most helpful and courageous. He told me of the best man for my purpose, but would not give me anything in writing; only a verbal message, which I had to repeat exactly.

The priest in question assured me that my son's faith was a matter of complete indifference to him. He would do whatever I asked, but I must obtain permission for him to visit my son in camp. He was not allowed to make priestly visitations to the prisoners unless the latter had urgently asked to see him. But even then such visits were often prevented. He had been told some time ago that the prisoners did not want any priestly exhortations. In one special case a Catholic woman had begged him to visit her husband, and he had made several attempts to do so, but on each occasion he had been told that the prisoner refused to see him; he was in no need of religious exhortations. Afterwards it was learned that the man had been most anxious to speak to the priest, but had simply been forbidden to see him.

This priest asked me to ascertain whether it was the truth that there were now no Catholic prisoners in the Lichtenberg camp, as the authorities declared. (A year later I was able to testify that there were Catholics in the camp.)

I went to several pastors, to whom I could plausibly introduce myself as the granddaughter of two Protestant clergymen. I learned that the Lichtenberg chaplain had been dismissed, and that his successor was a "German Christian."

Not until the 20th August was I able to pay the desired visit. My son assured me that things were going well with him. He walked a few steps, so that I could see that his leg was completely rigid; but at all events it was still there. I could see no traces of maltreatment, although I examined his head very thoroughly. I said, suddenly: "But how thin your hair is getting!"—and before the guard could prevent me I took his head between my hands and examined the back of it for bald spots. His head was almost close shaven, so that one could see the scalp.

Hans informed me, amongst other things, that at Papenburg he was told that he had been sentenced to ten years' detention in a concentration camp.

Not much could be said in a quarter of an hour, but my general impression was reassuring. When the time was up I had to leave the room, while my son remained there until someone came for him. The official in the adjoining room said to me: "There's no sense in your spending these minutes in separate rooms. You can stay with him until they come." And he let me go back to Hans. We were quite alone for a minute, and I learned that he truly had not been ill-treated, and that conditions were very much better than in his previous camps. I had time to whisper to him: "If you are ill-treated, sign yourself only 'Hans'!" He usually signed his letters to me with his full name, Hans Achim, while in writing to his friends he signed himself Hans.

After my return I wrote to Captain H., thanking him. I had convinced myself of the truth of what he had told me. I had come away with a favourable impression of my son's condition.

CHAPTER 11

Thoughts Are Free!

THE LETTERS WHICH I RECEIVED from the camp were quite contented in tone. I told my English friend, who was leaving for England, that my son was moderately well, and that his leg, although it was rigid, was still attached to his body.

While I was considering how I could possibly manage to see him again I was helped by a commission which Hans sent me through a liberated prisoner. He was a youth of the Berlin proletariat, and he was absolutely in rags when he came to see me. He explained that he had brought me a greeting from my son, and, opening his tattered jacket, he pointed to a woollen sweater. "My identification!" he said. It was a sweater that I had given to Hans, and which he had given to the youth, with the remark that he could send it back when he had got a warm coat again. I at once gave him my sweater in exchange.

This young man had been given his fare by Hans, and he told me how greatly Hans had always helped the other prisoners with the money which we sent him. At this time one could send a prisoner fifteen marks weekly. Hans began by asking us to send him a much smaller sum, but he was very soon glad to receive the maximum amount, as he gave a great deal of it to others.

The young man told me that there was a rumour to the effect that some of the prisoners would be going to Dachau. I must do my utmost to prevent this.

I therefore called on Captain H. again, having assured him over the telephone that I had no complaint to make, nor was I going to ask for a permit. I told him that a rumour was current in Berlin that several of the Lichten-burg prisoners were going to be transferred to Dachau, which was regarded as a particularly bad camp.

"No," he said, "if your son were coming to Dachau I should know of it already. Of course I cannot guarantee that such an order will not be given later. But nothing of the kind need be expected at present. It would not, however, be a misfortune, for Dachau is a model camp with admirable sanitary arrangements."

"The sanitary arrangements are not much help when one is tortured to death," I said.

"No, no!" he replied. "Definitely, there is no brutal-ity there."

"But you know what my son has suffered," I said, "and there are the most horrible rumours about Dachau."

"If there ever were brutalities there," he said, "which I really cannot believe, there are certainly none now. I inspected the camp only a fortnight ago, and I found that everything was excellent."

"That is not surprising," I retorted, "if one considers how such inspections are made. Since the camp receives notice of an inspection several days beforehand the staff have plenty of time to hide the ill-treated prisoners. You should take the camp by surprise; then you would be morely likely to realize what is going on."

"No, no!" he protested. "Definitely, such things don't happen any longer. You were able to convince yourself at Lichtenberg that all is well there; and when I was at Dachau I questioned a Communist, who told me that his treatment there was excellent."

"I suppose you know," I said, "that my son always told me how well he was treated, while one could actually see the traces of brutal handling. Such statements are absolutely valueless."

However, he was firmly convinced of the truth of the statement made by the man whom he had questioned, and who, "although he was a Communist," had made an excellent impression on him.

I referred once more to Lichtenburg, and thanked him again for his help in obtaining a permit. "You see how right it was to let me visit the camp. If one had more opportunities of convincing oneself of the health and comfort of prisoners there would be no false rumours. I sent word to England immediately that the report that my son had lost his leg was false, and that for the time being he is decently treated."

The mention of England seemed to make the captain nervous; he drummed on the table with his fingers and gave me a searching glance. I felt that I had been foolish to admit my relations with England. Somewhat intimidated, I explained: "I think I was perfectly right to do so; I personally believe it to be of the greatest importance that false rumours of atrocities should not be spread abroad, and I shall always be prepared to deny them."

Suddenly he gave me a most amiable smile. "How long was it since you had seen your son?" he asked. And when I replied: "Three months," he said: "Do you want to see him again? I am giving you a permit." After I had the permit safe I smiled, and said: "I should like to remind you once again that I have kept the promise which I gave you over the telephone: I have not asked for a permit. You have given me one of your own free will. I am obliged to say this, or it might be said afterwards that I had obtained an interview under false pretences!"

He promised me, as I took my leave, that I could obtain a permit from him every three months.

This time I was able to spend a whole hour with Hans, and so it continued for the next two years. I was very well satisfied with his condition. He assured me, in the most convincing terms, that he was going on very well indeed, and that I need have no anxiety.

In a hotel, where I waited until the omnibus started, by

cautiously sounding the proprietor and the hotel guests, I learned a good deal about the camp; and I was told that there was now a new commandant, a "very decent man," by the name of Reich.

Of course, my conversation with Hans took place in the presence of a guard, as usual, yet we managed on each occasion, by a sign or a few interjected words, to understand each other. Hans was keenly interested in anything I had to tell him about his friends. He himself spoke at great length, with every sign of interest, of his scientific work. Any mention of politics, or of anything relating to the camp, was forbidden.

Men began to call on me who had been in camp with Hans; in the same group, or even in the same cell. Only then did I learn that he was employed in the bookbinding department; for on my visits to the camp I was forbidden to question him as to his work. He was greatly liked and respected by all the prisoners, and even the more human of the SS men were impressed by his scholarship; indeed, he was regarded as a miracle of learning. The staff consulted him in respect of any legal difficulties. One man, after seeking his opinion, even asked Hans to represent him in court. He was greatly astonished when Hans told him that he could no longer practise as an advocate. The would-be client had supposed that whatever he, as an SS man, demanded would be granted.

Another guard consulted Hans in respect of an unhappy love-affair. Here, too, he could surely give a man good advice! Hans recommended him to read Rilke. He did read him diligently, coming to Hans for an explanation of the difficult passages. Whether this cured him of his trouble I never learned.

I also came to understand what letters from their relatives meant to the prisoners, and especially to Hans. They were read again and again: Hans could never bring himself to destroy them. In the Lichtenberg camp he and his trusted friends would often pore for hours over my letters, each of them examining every sentence, to determine whether it had a special significance.

Accordingly, writing to Hans became a carefully deliberate task, especially for Heinz, who was much cleverer than I at camouflaging a message. To begin with, the letters must interest Hans. I visited the exhibitions and gave detailed descriptions of what I saw, or I wrote of recent publications which might appeal to him. Any news of his old friends, or of fellow-prisoners who had been released, interested him keenly; especially news of their children, and their educational progress. Even in his last letter, written during the period of his most terrible experiences, he spoke of the importance of ensuring that the two-year-old son of his friend Sulamith, who showed signs of musical talent, should be prevented from hearing bad music. His favourites were the Fürsts' children; and next to them came the child of Walter and Sulamith, who was born in exile—in Spain. The children's mothers were touchingly anxious that I should give news of them in almost every letter, and enclose a photograph. This made the letters seem more innocuous. It might have annoyed the censor had we always spoken only of cultural matters.

Letters to Lichtenberg were supposed to contain only four pages. But when I learned that the censor "positively liked" reading my letters, because they were always so "frightfully interesting," and contained so many examples of childish wit or cleverness, I gradually increased them to eight pages; and in order that the censor should find it easier to read them I used a typewriter. He had said that he wished the use of a typewriter had been prescribed, as it made the work of censoring the letters so much easier.

Unfortunately this agreeable person was replaced by a new censor who was not at all pleased with my letters. One was returned to me, "because too long," and on others he wrote unamiable comments: "You had better send an art periodical at once!" I now had to restrict my letters to the regulation four pages, and as the number of prisoners increased the numbers of lines permitted was reduced.

On the outbreak of the civil war in Spain Hans became very anxious about his friends Walter and Sulamith. He took it for granted that they should fight for liberty and humanity. Walter, who was working for the Government as official photographer, had fastened to his revolver a tiny golden kitten, which Hans, when plead-ing in court, had carried on his person as a talisman. Was he not fighting in the same cause as Hans?—I had to tell this to Hans, and in order to do so I described Walter as fighting on the side of Franco. The notion of so disguising him made Hans burst into laughter—that care-free, boyish laughter that we all loved so, and which I never heard from him at any other time during his long imprisonment. I never told him how many of his friends, both men and women, had died fighting against the Fascist barbarians.

I heard of several prisoners who had been offered their freedom if they would pledge themselves to act as spies. Even in the camp a prisoner could make sure of better conditions by denouncing his fellows. This made life more difficult for the prisoners; they had always to be on their guard, for many hitherto decent men succumbed to temptation. When I asked my visitors: "Have they made this offer to Hans?" they looked at me in amazement: "No; no one has dared to make it to Hans."

I was told, further, that Hans was in some respects a privileged person. Even the commandant was im-pressed by his nobility of character, and had on several occasions recommended his release.

Hans had even found it possible to help other prisoners whose position was especially intolerable by asking that they should be transferred to the bookbinding department. This was under his management, and he was responsible for the good execution and punctual delivery of the work. No one asked him how he apportioned his time, so, apart from the official hours of leisure, he often found it possible to get on with his scientific work, for he was comparatively undisturbed in the quiet room. He sent for whole parcels of scientific books, which were often difficult to obtain, and rather expensive. At the same time, to my astonishment, he asked for a large number of detective-stories. I was told that these were used for "bribing" the SS men, who were very keen on them.

His favourite subject was medieval literature. He translated various works from the early High German, and he was working at a textbook for children of about fourteen, which would teach them something of the beauty of this literature. For this purpose he was comparing examples of the plastic arts and the literature of the period. The examples of literature were mostly taken from his own translations. As on leaving Lichtenburg he had to send all his possessions to me, I received, among other things, the draft of this anthology, in the comely black letters of the Stefan George books.

Hans was a strong educational influence among the prisoners of his group. He tried to ensure that each of them should continue his education, in accordance with his faculties; and for this purpose he even worked at subjects which did not interest him. For example, he sent for a mathematical textbook, in order to work through it with a student of physics who had been educated in one of the national schools.

Hans had often told me in his letters that he now had a delightful fellow-worker; this had cheered him greatly. I thought this companion must be a student of German philology, especially as a University professor, a teacher of philology, had assured me that my son could not possibly continue his study of the early Middle Ages without the necessary works of reference. At all events, his students would be unable to do so, even with a complete reference library. I learned afterwards that my son's companion was a mason, who had not the slightest previous knowledge of the subject, but had become passionately interested in it through listening to Hans.

Released prisoners from Lichtenberg kept on coming to see me. They were young men, often highly intelligent, and well educated, and always thoroughly sound in their way of thinking. They described the life in camp so exhaustively that I could picture it quite vividly. Those of them who lived in Berlin often came to see me, for Hans had impressed it upon me that I must keep an eye on them, and ensure that the intellectual interest which he had awakened in them was not allowed to decline. This, he thought, was most important, especially if they could not find employment.

One of them stayed with me for a few days on his way through Berlin. "I am really sorry that I have been discharged," he said. "Who will look after Hans now? He absolutely needs someone to look after him, and to see that his kindliness is not too badly abused. For example, when he buys food from the canteen—and they sell all sorts of provisions there—or offers the others coffee and cake on Sunday, he never eats anything himself, as the money is not enough to go round. I managed after a good deal of trouble to make sure that the others didn't eat until Hans had had something."

He had often made coffee for Hans in secret, or had prepared some little delicacy, and he was afraid that all this would stop now that he had left the camp. "If they had asked me whether I wanted to be released I should have said: 'No; I'd rather stay here as long as Hans is here.' Though, of course, if they were to ask me now—that is, now that I know what it is to be free again—I suppose I should say 'Yes.' "

When this young man left me his hands were trembling so that he could hardly pack his little trunk. I could see how he dreaded going out into the world. Perhaps he already guessed how difficult life can be for the liberated prisoner. The commandant used to tell the prisoners, on their discharge, that they would now be readmitted to the community of the workers and of the people; that they had served their sentence, and no one would remind them of their past. I am sure that Reich believed what he said (he was the only irreproachable commandant of whom I have ever heard). But most of the wretched prisoners were soon to learn better. This young man, like so many others, was absolutely unable to find work on leaving camp. If he had not been helped by genuine "Volksgenossen" he would have starved to death, since for some reason or other he had no unemployment pay.

He told me, when he came to Berlin again some time later: "When I informed people that I had been in camp with Hans Litten they listened to me. And since I was able to convince them, by what I had to tell them, that I knew him intimately, they absolutely spoiled me. I had a hot meal almost every day, for someone would nearly always invite me to dinner; I was given a warm overcoat, and anything else I needed. But I know very well that I owed these things merely to the fact that Hans had thought me worthy of his friendship."

One day a woman came to see me. There was great uneasiness among the people; and there was a rumour that Hans had been shot in reprisal for the murder of Gustloff. This woman had offered to come to see me on the pretext of bringing me a shirt of my son's. She had often mended his clothes in the past, and this garment had remained on her hands. I was able to reassure her; Hans was not in any trouble; I had just received a letter from him, which I showed to her. She must pass on the news at once, for I would not have had my son the subject of lying propaganda.

She spent the whole afternoon with me. We spoke only of Hans, whom she adored. After some enthusiastic remark of hers, I said: "I am always being told that in North Berlin there are many people who worship Hans as though he were a saint." She gave me a reproving glance, and said, with emphasis: "He *is* a saint!"

But I had other news of my son, which described not the kindly, helpful Hans Litten, but the fighter. Here is a sketch which I received from one W. S.

"In the middle of July 1934 all the inmates of the Oranienburg concentration camp were transferred to Lichtenberg (Saxony). It was said that we should meet a few old acquaintances, a few 'notables' there; but it was generally supposed that Hans Litten was still in Esterwegen-Papenburg. However, at this time he was already at Lichtenberg, though we did not know this until we left the cells of the concentration camp for the common rooms. What a state we found him in! Comrades who had seen him in Brandenburg camp, where he had made a good recovery from the brutal maltreatment which he had suffered previously, hardly recognized him; and on us, who had never encountered him during his imprisonment, he made a deep impression. With shaven head, supporting himself on two sticks, a pale, slender apparition, only his eyes were living; they gazed at us attentively through his spectacles. Some of us were strangers; some he hardly knew; others he knew well; but he shook hands with us all just as cordially, greeting us as friends. He was at once the centre of the company.

Of what he had endured he did not care to speak. His back was bowed a little—but not his spirit.

"In Lichtenberg he was comparatively comfortable. He was occupied in the bookbinding department, and he also had charge of the library. This post suited him admirably; he was able to advise us in our reading, recommending this book, advising us against that. . . .

"Delighted to see him, yet shocked by his appearance, we often used to speak to Litten. He was lodged in the opposite building, which we could not enter except when changing our books. He enjoyed his task as librarian. It was said, however, that he had suffered horribly during the early part of his time in Lichtenberg; for his damaged leg and his stiff knee did not prevent the SS men from tormenting him. I think the period of which I am speaking, when he was busy binding or distributing books, was the happiest time of his imprisonment.

"Brandenburg lay behind him, and Esterwegen; now it was Lichtenberg. One may well wonder how this not particularly robust human being found the strength to challenge his enemies even in this horrible captivity. He did it as follows:

"Some sort of Nazi celebration was made a pretext for driving all the prisoners into one large hall. They were given the order to 'celebrate.' And they celebrated; the prisoners themselves devised the programme, and they themselves had to supply the items. This was difficult enough for men who were naturally afraid of getting into trouble if they did not make use of definitely Nazi material. Hans Litten saw a way out; he found some book of poems in his library, and selected pieces were recited. Hans Litten took his turn, and we all stood listening intently to his poem. We were deeply moved when he had ended his recitation. He had the pluck to recite, in the presence of the SS, a poem which we had sung over and over again in the *Jugendbewegung*:

Die Gedanken sind frei,[1]

Wer kann sie erraten,
Sie fliegen vorbei
Wie nächtliche Schatten.
Kein Mensch kann sie
    wissen,
Kein Jäger erschiessen,
Es bleibet dabei:
Die Gedanken sind frei.

Ich denke was ich will,
Und was mich beglücket,

Doch alles in der Still
Und wie es sich schicket.
Mein Wunsch und
     Begehren
Kann niemand verwehren,
Es bleibet dabei:
Die Gedanken sind frei.

Und sperrt man mich ein
In finstere Kerker,
Das alles sind rein

[1] Thoughts are free
Who can guess them?
They fly past
Like evening shadows.
No man can know them,
No hunter shoot them:
One thing is sure:
Thoughts are free.

I think what I will
And what rejoices me:
Yet all in silence
As is befitting.

My wish and my longing
Can none forbid:
One thing is sure:
Thoughts are free.

Though they shut me up
In a dungeon dark
All this is vain
Availing them nothing;
For then my thoughts
Shiver the bolts
And shatter the walls:
Thoughts are free!

Vergebliche Werke,   Und Mauern entzwei:
Denn meine Gedanken   Die Gedanken sind frei!
Zerreissen die Schranken

"The SS did not grasp the meaning of the poem or the speaker's intention; or they understood them only when it was too late.

"Just think: All around were black uniforms worn by SS men of the killer type; in front of us, overlooking us a little, stood a poor, crippled, tortured human being. And suddenly he read a poem which in these surroundings had a revolutionary, indeed an inflammatory effect. For all of us this was an event! It called for personal courage, and it was this that made Hans Litten so hated by the Nazis; they hated him because his inmost self was unbroken."

CHAPTER III

Friendship

FOR HIS LITERARY WORK Hans needed the *Muspilli*,
which he wanted to translate. Since I could not find a
copy of this poem, a specialist in old High German literature removed it from a very valuable work. Heinz, to
whom he gave these pages, made no secret of his astonishment that the scholar should have dissected this costly
book for a total stranger. The professor replied: "I assure you, for your brother I would have a piece of flesh
cut out of my body, if I could help him by so doing.
Shall I hesitate to cut up a valuable book in order to give
him pleasure?"

Such proofs of friendship from total strangers, which
I reported to Hans when I saw him, were a great consolation to him. And they meant a very great deal to him.
I have always been told that prisoners, even after a short
term of captivity, begin to feel that they are forgotten
and forsaken. I hope my son never felt this.

It interested me to see how tradespeople reacted if I
said that I was buying something for my son. At the
bookseller's when I bought books for him the assistants

took the greatest trouble to find what I wanted, which was not always easy, sending for catalogue after catalogue, making long abstracts, and even offering their own copies if the book was out of print. "I would never have parted with this particular copy, but since it is for your son . . . !"

Shortly before Christmas a propaganda speech was broadcast, in which the speaker raged against that enemy of the people, Hans Litten. I was told that the salespeople in a certain shop were still working after the doors were closed, so that they were obliged to listen to this instructive broadcast. When the name of Hans Litten fell on their ears they all like one man spontaneously stopped their work and did not stir until the end of the broadcast: as though they were honouring a hero.

The second-hand bookseller to whom I went with a long list of books that I wanted him to find for me said: "What an amazingly learned man he must be who compiled this list of books!"—"This man," I replied, "is in a concentration camp; and he drew up the list in camp, without any outside help." As he was listening with great interest I continued: "Perhaps you would like to know his name. He is my son, the barrister Hans Litten."

At this he was almost beside himself with excitement. "I don't want any money from him!" he cried, and he laid the amount of his profit on the counter. "You must come to me with all your requirements. I shall take the greatest trouble to procure the most unobtainable books, and I don't want to make a penny by it!"

A genuine friendship sprang up between us, but one day the shop was empty, and it was impossible to learn what had become of the bookseller.

Once an itinerant bookseller stopped his heavily-laden barrow outside my house. "I've been told Hans Litten wants some light literature for the camp. Here's a little present from me." And he gave me some two hundred books.

I once asked a publisher if he would supply me at the trade price with an expensive book which Hans needed. He sent me not only this, but some twenty other interesting books on his list as a present for Hans.

A fruiterer's shop having attracted me by its wonderful display, I went in to buy some fruit, as I wanted to send a hamper to the camp. We were allowed to send parcels of food to Lichtenberg at Christmas, Easter, and Whitsun, and also on my son's birthday. The weight was not supposed to exceed ten pounds, but the inspectors were not very strict on this point. I gradually increased the weight up to twenty-five pounds; I knew that there would not be very much left for Hans, as he shared everything with his friends. I often wondered why he wanted an especially expensive cigarette—for I knew that he did not smoke—or for some delicacy for which he had never cared. But the liberated prisoners who came to see me would explain: "You know, that was for me. Hans had such a delightful way of discovering, quite unobtrusively, just what would please one best."

In the fruiterer's shop I said: "Please look out the very best fruit, and the soundest, so that it will keep. It is going to a concentration camp, and I don't know how long it may lie about before it is delivered."

The assistant bestirred herself at once, and when I told her that the hamper was for Hans Litten she gave a cry of delight, exclaiming: "Then there's simply nothing that's good enough! He got my husband out of trouble once!"

She carefully examined every single purchase, and then added some especially fine specimens on her own account. It was all I could do to prevent her from enclosing a *billet doux*. As a kind of ginger of which Hans was particularly fond was no longer obtainable, owing to the financial slump, the small remaining stock was removed from the shelves and reserved for my consignments.

My friends thought it foolish of me to make propaganda in this way, warning me that I might one day light upon a convinced Nazi. But I never once encountered any trace of disrespect when I asked for anything to be sent to "Hans Litten in the concentration camp."

CHAPTER IV

Lord Allen of Hurtwood and Herr von Ribbentrop

OF COURSE, at every opportunity that offered I interceded for my son with the heads of the State—Hitler, Göring, Himmler, and Hindenburg. I applied also to the various personal adjutants, and to people like Hess. I did this on special occasions, on Hitler's birthday, on Nazi anniversaries, and when the Government had brought off a coup of any kind. My appeals took every imaginable form; some contained a full justification of my request, others were brief and urgent, and after the plebiscite in the Saar I even telegraphed my petition. Generally speaking I received a polite refusal; sometimes it was laconic, sometimes reasons were given to justify the refusal; sometimes the reply was telephoned. At last I was informed that my appeals would remain unanswered if I wrote so often; I had the right to submit a petition once in three months; so I confined myself to these quarterly appeals.

Once the Gestapo asked me to call, and a Government official informed me that they could not release my son, as his life would not be safe if he were at large.

I: "I shall see that he is safe, if only he is let out of camp."

He: "He might be killed in the street one day, and then there would be more indignation abroad."

I: "If you are afraid of indignation abroad I can only advise you to release my son. A man may be killed in the street in any part of the world; no one would see cause for special indignation in that. But the fact that you are slowly torturing your prisoners to death in your camps is a thing that fills the whole civilized world with indignation."

He: "I didn't hear what you have just said."

I: "Then I'll repeat it."

He: "No, that you shall not! I *must* not hear what you have just said. Apart from that, your son is a person of intellectual consequence, and therefore a dangerous enemy. If he were released he would work against us."

I: "Not if he pledged himself to abstain from doing so. But you can send him straight across the frontier; then you would have nothing more to fear."

He: "Isn't it the truth that he would work against us, abroad? We have had enough experience of that sort of thing."

I: "But if I remain in this country you have a hostage. My son would never open his lips if he knew that I were in your hands. You can insure yourself against danger by interning me."

He (very dignified) : "We have risen above the medieval device of arresting hostages."

I could have mentioned a whole series of cases in which the Nazis were not above this practice, but I did not wish to anger him needlessly, so I merely said: "If anyone offers herself voluntarily as a hostage, that is quite a different matter." I asked him whether, if my son could not be released, he might not at least be confined in a different manner: for example, he could be interned in a fortress. And I particularized the frightful brutalities which Hans had suffered.

He: "You must not say such things!"

"But they are true!" I cried; and I cited various conversations with officials, who themselves admitted the brutalities.

He (in a menacing tone) : "Would your memory of what you are asserting be so accurate if it should come to an inquiry?"

I: "Of course! I shall never, to the Day of Judgment, forget a single word that has been said or a single act that has been committed. Whether the officials would remember their conversation so accurately is another question."

He (threateningly) : "Will you persist in what you have said if you are *seriously* questioned?"

"To the last drop of my blood," I replied.

He rose to his feet. "I cannot listen to what you are saying. And it is useless for you to tell me all this; I can do nothing for you. In this case I am only an instrument. I shall forget what you have said; that is the only thing I can do for you."

He shook hands with me, and I left him.

A friend of mine induced the Secretary of State, Meissner, to present a petition of mine to Hindenburg, and to give it his support. In this petition I gave full details of my son's case, and I reminded Hindenburg of the manner in which he had shown his appreciation of my husband, during and after the war. Meissner wrote that Hindenburg had listened to the petition with great sympathy and had forwarded it to the competent authority. —Result: it was rejected, like the rest of my petitions.

At the Gestapo I referred one day to Hindenburg's attitude toward my son's case. "I am very sorry," said Himmler's adjutant, "but in this matter even the good Papa Hindenburg is powerless.

Another day, running his fingers through his hair in desperation, he cried: "How happy I should be if I could tell you: Your son is coming out!"

Once, when I mentioned in the course of a conversation that my son had come to grips with Hitler in a court of law, he said, with a startled expression: "Then, of course, it's useless to think of his ever being liberated."

"What!" I cried, in feigned astonishment: "even you think the Führer capable of such behaviour? Then is it possible that all those people are right who explain my son's martyrdom by this encounter?   I have always told them: you can't possibly accuse the Führer of the German people of such a petty, vulgar, base lust of vengeance!"

"No, no!" he cried.   "Naturally, that's quite out of the question. Of course the Führer is not revengeful. I only meant that one thing adds up to another, and this would make your son's release more difficult."

From another source I heard that there was a list of prisoners who were not to be released under any circumstances. In their case nothing could be done without the Führer's consent. The list included the name of Hans Litten.

I learned also that my son's dossier at the Gestapo included a picture which showed him as counsel for the defence and Hitler as witness, facing each other in court.

Captain H. rather liked to hear me make a political observation from time to time, as he imagined that my attitude was "fanatically Nationalistic." He may have considered that my rejection of National Socialism was sufficiently explained by my personal experiences. I suppose he attributed my intercession for the "Communist scoundrels," to which he often incited me, to mere political inexperience. For he was quite willing to believe that I was no politician; the more so as I always declared that in judging a man the first thing to be considered was his character.

Once, when I had somewhat incautiously ventured to

express a political opinion, he said, in the kindest manner, but with an undertone of warning: "I believe we should have done well to lock up this charming little mother, too."

This was quite agreeable to me. "But I am always telling you it would be much better to lock me up and let my son go free. I am the person responsible, since I brought up my son to be such a decent human being that you find him insupportable."

He exclaimed, in alarm: "For God's sake! There you are again, with your favourite theme! I have told you a hundred times already, that is not possible!"

I wrote to Frau Sonnemann, who was then on the Obersalzberg with Göring. I had never heard from her since our interview; nevertheless, I was anxious to make another attempt to enlist her sympathy. I told her I had the feeling that my petitions had never reached the proper authority, and I begged her to tell me how I could make sure that my appeal would really be placed in Göring's hands. I enclosed a draft of a petition which I wanted to send, in order to ask her whether it was expressed in the proper form.

A few weeks later she rang me up: "My dear Frau Litten, don't be angry with me for not replying to you sooner, but I expect you will have heard of our motor-car accident on the Obersalzberg. I have only just returned to Berlin, and I am still suffering from an injury to the knee."

I assured her of my sympathy and concern—which was genuine, for I liked this kindly woman—to which she replied: "Oh, it doesn't matter about me. The important thing is that Göring is improving."

"But the newspapers say that he is quite right again!"

"That," she said, "is only to reassure the public; the people would be so terribly concerned. He was much more seriously hurt than was admitted. The steering-wheel crushed his chest when the cars collided, and injured him very badly. For the rest, I gave your petition to Göring. It arrived as we were sitting at breakfast. He read it, and all he said was: 'A pity Frau Litten tells such lies. She declares that her son did not belong to the Communist Party. Of course he did.' I said: 'I know Frau Litten, and I think it quite out of the question that she should be lying.' He said: 'Well, then she doesn't know the facts,' and asked the other gentlemen who were sitting at table. They said: 'Of course Litten is a Communist. He was even a Reichstag deputy,' and they could actually refer to the sessions in which he and Göring went for each other."

"They are confusing him with someone else!" I exclaimed. "I really must have known it if my son had ever been a deputy! And here I can give you proof."

"No, no!" she replied. "Your word is enough. Of course I'll explain the matter to Göring at once, although he has forbidden me ever to mention your son to him again. These were his very words: 'If you go on dinning

Litten into my ears I'll have nothing more to do with you'; and you see, that would be very regrettable, for then I could no longer help anyone."

I obtained from the office of the Reichstag a certificate to the effect that during my son's life there had never been a deputy to the Reichstag bearing the name of Litten.   I could not obtain evidence that he had never belonged to the Communist Party, since the office of the K.P.D. was no longer in existence.

A few days later one of Göring's adjutants rang me up and informed me that my petition had been rejected.   I told him that this rejection must surely be based upon the mistaken belief that my son had been a Communist deputy to the Reichstag.   I had just obtained proof of the contrary from the office of the Reichstag.   But he replied: "That has been cleared up in the meantime.   We know that was a misunderstanding.   But that doesn't alter the case."

Finding myself in Geneva, I took the opportunity of getting into touch with Professor Burckhardt, who had been in Germany on the business of the Red Cross.

We met in a café, and sat in a sheltered alcove.   When I began to tell him of all sorts of atrocities, he suddenly asked his secretary to inspect the adjacent alcoves.   To my astonished exclamation: "But we are not in Germany!" he replied: "The Gestapo have their spies here, just as in your country, and it might be very unpleasant for you if our conversation were overheard."

He told me that he had had occasion to visit Lichtenburg, and that he had spoken to my son. His impression of the place (he saw it when Reich was commandant) was favourable as compared with that of other camps, and he reported that he had been impressed by the perfect discipline prevailing there.

He told me that during his visit to Germany he had procured the release of quite a number of inoffensive prisoners, but his efforts on my son's behalf were fruitless. His only achievement in respect of the more prominent prisoners was to get Ossietzky removed from the camp to a hospital, as he was to all appearances dying.

From other people, too, more numerous than I can mention, I received the most unselfish assistance. We were working from three centres. Heinz went to Prague and to Holland and I to Switzerland. Our visits did not excite suspicion, for Heinz had friends in Prague and in Holland, while I went to see Rainer.

Both individuals and organized bodies came to our assistance. But of them I can say nothing; I should imperil the one and hinder the devoted labours of the other.

Captain H. gave me some advice in respect of a petition to Himmler, which he himself presented. When I told him one day, in conversation, that my son was absolutely no politician, but a scholar pure and simple, and explained the nature of his work, which was a sufficient proof that he did not concern himself with politics, he said: "Ah, Germanic art. Of course—the excavations that Himmler is so interested in. Perhaps one could draw his attention to that."

I gave him a translation of the Wessobrunner prayer, with my son's extremely learned commentary, and he passed it on to Himmler, who would not have understood it, nor would it have made any impression on him. Some little time later Captain H. rang me up and said: "Gracious lady, I'm most awfully sorry, but this petition, too, has been rejected. You will hardly be surprised if you have read yesterday's newspapers."

"Yes," I said; "the news yesterday was frightful, and everything sounds so hopeless that I wish I could see my son and console him."

He thought this natural, and gave me a permit at once, though this was in the interval between the regulation visits.

The newspapers had reported that Lord Allen of Hurtwood had sent a petition to Hitler, which was signed by a number of the most eminent English lawyers, praying for the release of Hans Litten. There were no further details of this communication. I knew, however, that the Litten case had appealed to the sympathies of the English lawyers, and of the barristers in particular, because an attempt had been made to force a barrister to violate his professional secrecy. The document appar-

ently laid stress upon this fact, and insisted on the absolute innocence of the prisoner.

After Hans had been tortured, and had then attempted
to kill himself, Margot had secretly crossed the frontier.
She had spent a few weeks in Prague and in Switzerland,
in order to interest foreign sympathizers in the case, and
to publish in the Press a report of what had happened.
It was only then that the outer world became aware of
the case; but now there were repeated references to it
in the Press, and even in the great English Conservative
newspapers.

Lord Allen's appeal was answered by Ribbentrop.

Berlin, 16th December, 1935.

Sehr verehreter Lord Allen!

Your letter of the 31st October to the Führer and
Reichskanzler was forwarded to me by the Chancellery
for further consideration, and on account of an accumu-
lation of work I am only to-day able to reply to it.

To begin with, I must inform you that after careful
examination of the case which you particularize I am to
my regret unable to recommend to the Führer and
Reichskanzler the solution which you propose. The reasons for this are as follows:

The barrister Hans *Litten was one of the intellectual
leaders of Communism in Germany.* He is interned on
account of treasonable activity, and his intellectual stand-
point makes it impossible to release him under present
circumstances.

The statements made in the petition of your legal

friends are partly founded upon *false hypotheses* and are partly *at variance with the facts*, and for this reason cannot be left unrefuted. Revolutions are not fought out in the courts of law and in accordance with the rules of normal legal procedure, and for the rest, the treatment of the barrister Litten, despite your assertion to the contrary, is absolutely irreproachable, and I am told that he actually enjoys certain special privileges.

But now, my dear Lord Allen, I should like for my own part to ask you: Can a Government, and with it a legal system, which places behind bolt and bar the incorrigible enemies of human society who wished to deliver a people over to Communism—can it really be such a bad legal system if it thereby at the same time restores a nation of sixty-five millions to happiness? Does humanity exist for the law, or does the law exist for humanity? Should such a legal system really be perpetually concerned about the world's opinion of it?

On the other hand, as against this I should like to make the assertion: if your English lovers of justice who have signed this petition would take the trouble to study the causes of the decline of my country since 1919, since the Versailles Treaty, they would find that an unprogressive administration of justice, which was no longer equal to dealing with the stupendous problems of our age, and above all the spirit in which the law was often administered, and whose representatives, against the natural temper of the German people, could judge the protagonist of liberty, Adolf Hitler, under the same statute as the Communist Hans Litten, had also contributed to lead a great nation to the verge of the abyss, that is, of Communism.

That we to-day are no longer disposed to allow this spirit ever to raise its head again in Germany, and that we so far as possible restrict the field of action of incorrigible representatives and intellectual leaders of such nihilism as persons dangerous to human society would be understood by any of your friends of the legal faculty if he had lived in Germany during the developments of the fourteen years ending 30th January, 1933. Indeed, what is more, I am firmly convinced that Great Britain and the whole civilized world must one day be grateful to Adolf Hitler in that he has isolated with iron consistency, and where need be with severity, the representatives in Germany of this creeping and corroding Communist poison.

In future Germany is to be a constitutional State in true concordance with the nature of the German people and its sense of justice. This is the endeavour of those who are seeking to create a new National Socialist German legislation.

During the next few days I will take the liberty of sending you the latest foreign edition of the proceedings of the *Akademie für Deutsches Recht*, containing a brief introduction by myself, and I believe that it would contribute greatly to mutual understanding if your legal friends would establish a vivifying contact with our Academy and its director, Reichsminister Dr. Frank.

For the rest, there is one other matter to which I must allude. The greatest intellectual revolution in the history of the German people, which led up to the seizure of power by National Socialism on the 30th January, 1933, was effected under conditions of complete legality, and brought to a conclusion by methods which are quite unprecedented in history, and which are in violent con-

trast to the cruel and barbarous methods by which the revolutions of other peoples of our civilization have been effected.

I do not think I am a false prophet when I say that the objective historiography of the future will one day regard the National Socialist struggle for power as the pattern example of a revolution, such as can be effected only by a nation of the highest cultural standards.

Can there be a better proof of this than the fact that a great international historian recently told us in all earnestness that the world would certainly have had a better comprehension of the National Socialist revolution if it had been accomplished by the cruel and barbarous methods of earlier revolutions?

Apart from the fundamental considerations just mentioned, I am all the less able to decide upon taking a positive attitude toward the desires of your honourable legal friends inasmuch as in a similar case we had a very unfortunate experience. This was as follows:

Some time ago one of your countrymen, an eminent Englishman, asked me to consider how great an obstacle in the way of a German-English understanding was the imprisonment of the Bulgarians, Dimitroff and his comrades, known to the world through the Reichstag fire trial, and what an excellent impression their release would make on English public opinion. I knew that here we were dealing with incorrigible enemies of human social order, and that it would be best if they were never again let loose on humanity. Despite this, or rather in my constant endeavour to promote German-English understanding, I became an advocate of their liberation. The Bulgarians were sent to Russia, and today Dimitroff *is Secretary-General and thereby the true leader of the Komintern! He is one of the most inveterate Communists and pestilent terrorists, who at the 7th Congress of the Komintern in Moscow last summer confessed to approximately the following aims:*

(1) The immovable aim of the Komintern is the world revolution and the establishment of the dictatorship of the proletariat. To achieve this aim all means are proper: alliances, propaganda, terror, violence, etc.

(2) The greatest obstacle in the way of world revolution —namely, the establishment of Red imperialism—is Adolf Hitler. For this reason National Socialism must be fought with all means. If Hitler-Germany falls the road is clear for the Communistic world-rule. In a little while all Europe will follow, and the disintegration of the British Empire and the still surviving national States will irresistibly follow.

This charming programme is the result of Dimitroff's release: that is, the outcome of the Liberal, British conception of the world and of German kindliness and magnanimity! As a matter of curiosity I ought at least to add that at the time I notified his English advocates of his liberation, but that neither they nor the public opinion and the press of England, which had previously been so terribly agitated over the case of the Bulgarians, took the slightest notice of this fact. *I think such mistakes should be avoided by both nations in future.*

My dear Lord Allen! Your hostility towards Versailles is known to Germany and the world, and your advocacy of a German-English friendship has always been a great satisfaction to me in my own (I think not quite unknown) campaign for this friendship. I know, therefore, that only noble motives have actuated you and your friends in your petition of the 31st October to the Führer and Reichskanzler.

We Germans understand this British feeling "for the under-dog" very well, and respect it, as it must indeed be the case in members of the same race. But this very sense of solidarity in people of the same race and the same blood ought to be a guarantee of the common recognition that the *raison d'état* of governments often compels them to follow harsh courses, although the people does not thereby abandon the least fraction of its ethical and philosophical foundation, based upon its inmost nature; indeed, on the contrary, these harsh courses are often the very conditions of preserving this ethical and moral basis of the people. Modern England has hitherto been somewhat lacking in recognition of this fact. I believe, however, that these ideas will become more generally accepted from day to day, and here the history of the British Empire should be the best teacher!

Inasmuch as I hope that I shall still often have the pleasure of meeting you on the path that leads to German-English friendship, please be assured, my dear Lord Allen, of the highest esteem and the friendliest feelings

Of yours faithfully,

VON RIBBENTROP.

This letter sounded as though the Government meant to imprison my son for life. In a petition to Ribbentrop I refuted his preposterous assertions sentence by sentence. I never received any reply.

When I went to see Hans in Lichtenberg two days later he was greatly surprised to receive a visit between the regulation dates. I explained that I had been afraid that he would have been depressed by the reports in the newspapers, and that I had wanted to encourage and console him. He replied that he had been greatly distressed on my account, but that he himself had no hopes whatever of imminent release. On this occasion everyone behaved very kindly to me, and I was able to ask Hans under my breath whether the report in the Press had caused him suffering. No, he said; but I must continue to do what I could with foreign countries. This visit was very enjoyable. I tried to take this opportunity of speaking to the commandant. A comrade of my son's who had been released had told me that Hans often suffered so severely from spasms of the heart that he fell to the ground unconscious. I had written to the commandant, saying that a released prisoner had informed me as to the state of my son's health, and I begged that he might be given convalescent leave from the camp. The commandant thereupon had Hans examined by the camp doctor, and on writing to me he assured me that Hans was not in any way unfit for internment, but that in consideration of the state of his health he would be given lighter work.

The commandant sent word that he was too unwell to see me, but that I was to say what I wished to the adjutant. I told him that I had come on account of the report in the Press, every sentence of which was inaccurate; above all, the description of my son as a dangerous enemy of human society was absolutely false. I was afraid that the staff of the camp would be influenced by this description rather than by their personal knowledge of my son. I was anxious, therefore, to correct this impression, and I took it upon myself to offer him a copy of my letter to Ribbentrop. He refused to read it, however; explaining that the commandant of a camp did not ask what a man had done, or what he was. All that concerned him was how the man behaved himself in the camp. For the rest, he was greatly displeased by the statement in Ribbentrop's letter, to the effect that my son was enjoying certain special privileges. Under his command there were no such things as special privileges. All the prisoners received the same treatment. Had my son ever spoken of any special privileges, and had I repeated what he told me to other people?—I replied that I had never heard any mention of special privileges, whether from my son or from discharged prisoners. But I myself had been extremely gratified to read of them in Ribbentrop's letter. It had seemed to me only right, and indeed a matter of course, that men who had been so long in the camp, and had behaved so well, should be given certain privileges. —No, said the commandant; such a thing was out of the question. But he was very amiable, so that I really had the impression that the staff had a kindly feeling for Hans.

I heard afterwards, from one of the discharged prisoners, that Lord Allen's petition had impressed the SS men; they felt that Hans must be treated with special regard. And later on, when Lord Allen was the Führer's guest in Nuremberg, the general opinion in the camp was "that there must, of course, be something special about Litten, when so famous a man as Lord Allen, who is actually invited to Nuremberg as the Führer's guest, is so interested in his case."

Apart from this, I was told repeatedly by discharged prisoners that all efforts to arouse opinion in foreign countries were of the very greatest service. Even when they did not result in the liberation of the prisoner, he was always better treated for a time. The camp authorities were always afraid that one of the foreigners interested in the case might visit the camp and ask to see the person for whom he was interceding, so that the prisoner in question must be kept in a fairly good condition.

Such motives, however, were not operative under Commandant Reich, for in his time the treatment of the prisoners, so far as he was responsible for it, was not inhuman. He insisted on the strictest discipline, as regards both the staff and the prisoners, so that no improper treatment of the latter was possible. Of course, the prisoners were not always in a position to report improper treatment.

I know that Hans was greatly taken aback when a certain Remmert made his appearance in Lichtenberg, and at once began to shout at him in the most brutal fashion. This man had ill-treated Hans abominably at Esterwegen, and when "important visitors" came to the camp he recommended himself to them by his brutal treatment of the prisoners, including Hans.

Hans considered whether he should ask to see the commandant. He knew that Reich would intervene, but he did not venture to complain. "It is possible," he told himself, "that Remmert will be here longer than the commandant, for we know that in the Third Reich the disreputable elements retain their positions longer than the decent people. And if that were so he would find the means of revenging himself." So he said nothing, and Remmert soon mended his ways, when he saw that the commandant was determined to put down brutality of any kind.

CHAPTER V

The Plebiscite in Camp

HANS' LEG began to improve slightly. He had treated the kneejoint himself with vigorous flexion exercises and massage, and he said to me one day: "The doctor who treated me in Papenburg would never believe I could have done my knee so much good with energetic self-treatment."

One day, to my delight, Hans asked me for two framed pictures—reproductions of the Bamberg equestrian statue and the Uta in the Naumburg cathedral—and some stuff for a tablecloth and a curtain.

I learned from liberated prisoners that those who had been a long while in custody were paired off and lodged in cells of their own, which they were allowed to make as comfortable as circumstances permitted. This arrangement was especially convenient for Hans, as during his free time he could retire to his cell and devote himself to his literary work.

But he did not enjoy this luxury long. About two months later he wrote: "I am sending you shortly a package containing all the superfluous things I have here, including the cloth and the pictures and all superfluous books." I was to send him no more books, nor anything else for which he had not expressly asked.

He told me, too, that he had been transferred to another company. On my next visit his condition impressed me as anything but satisfactory. I could not discover what was wrong, but the whole atmosphere of the place was different.

This was just before the elections, and I whispered to him, during our interview: "Mind you vote 'Yes.' He looked at me as though I was demanding an utter absurdity, so directly it was safe to whisper again I said: "You simply must vote 'Yes.' I know what I'm talking about."

It had struck me that Hans was no longer using a stick. When I questioned him he replied that his leg was so well that he did not need a stick any longer. But I heard from released prisoners that Remmert had taken his stick away from him. Hans had reported this to the camp doctor, as he still urgently needed the stick; his knee was still so stiff that on going upstairs he had to step up with the good leg and drag the other after him. The doctor declared that he must make inquiry of the doctor at the Papenburg hospital before he could give orders that he was to use a stick again. His letter had to go through the office, and there it was simply held up. The doctor did not trouble to take any further steps, so that Hans had to do as best he could without a stick.

The next few letters from Hans gave me reason to suspect that conditions had altered for the worse. He had been separated from his best friend, which apparently distressed him greatly.

I went all over Berlin in search of someone who had recently been released from Lichtenberg, and at last I heard of a man who had left the camp since these recent changes. It was difficult to get hold of him; for he was terribly afraid of having anything to do with me. I tried walking past the office where his fiancée was employed, but I could never catch her; probably my behaviour attracted her attention. At last I was able, through a chance acquaintance, to persuade him to come and see me.

He told me that he was under observation, so that he had to be extremely cautious; he made a rule of never mentioning the camp in any way, but with Hans Litten's mother he felt that it was his duty to make an exception.

He told me that Hans had just had a terrible time with the camp dentist. He was quite a tolerable dentist, though not particularly gentle. But one had to have plenty of money if one wanted any sort of dental treatment. If a prisoner went to him with a violent toothache he had to pay him beforehand; if he had no money the tooth was simply drawn then and there; so much the dentist was obliged to do, but he would do nothing else without payment.

What I wanted above all to know was why there had been such a sudden change for the worse in the prisoners' condition. To begin with, he said, there was a new commandant, who was much harsher than the old one. Also some copies of an illegal newspaper had been found in the camp; there was nothing momentous in it, but its discovery was made a pretext for an exhaustive search through all the prisoners' possessions. Anything that was not a structural necessity had to go: the pictures on the walls, tablecloths and curtains, even the rugs with which some of the prisoners had carpeted their little rooms; and all books had to be given up.

Further, my informant said that at the time of the plebiscite a few of the prisoners had given their vote in the negative. The ballot was not really secret, and the dissenters had been transferred to a penal company, in which they were terribly oppressed and overworked.

Himmler himself had visited the camp, and had ordered that all who were serving a second term of detention were to be placed in a special company, in which they were abominably treated. My son's companion, for example, who was not only in camp for the second time, but had also voted in the negative, was transferred to the penal company. Hans had received no voting-paper; my informant could not tell me why.

I complained to Captain H. that conditions were worse in the camp, and that my son seemed terribly depressed. His health was obviously deteriorating.

Captain H. admitted that the camp was under harsher discipline. It was just that a few swine had been behaving badly. Anything of that sort was always followed by harsher measures. Unfortunately the innocent had to suffer with the guilty; there was no getting out of that. I must tell my son to keep his spirits up. He would give me a permit every second month.

I had already paid two visits to the camp at intervals of two months. On my third visit, as I was making my way to the office in which the permits were made out, a Gestapo official spoke to me in the lobby. I had never had any dealings with this man, though I had often seen him.

"Frau Litten," he said, "you are going to Lichtenberg too often."

"I naturally go there," I replied, "as often as I am given permission."

"The ordinary maximum is one permit a quarter. You have managed to go much oftener, and there has been trouble about it downstairs. I can't tell you anything, and no one must know that I've spoken to you. But listen to me—don't go oftener than once every quarter."

"But," I exclaimed, "Captain H. has just promised me that I can pay my next visit at Christmas; that is, in seven weeks' time. I can't make fresh arrangements now."

"You take my advice," he said, "and don't go again for three months!"

I had no intention of taking his advice; but my husband thought I had better do so. He knew, from his experience as a soldier, that subordinate officers often have more influence than their superiors. At all events, they could cause me a great deal of vexation if I got the wrong side of them, and they remained much longer in the same post than their superiors. A personal adjutant did not usually retain his appointment for years. I saw the force of this, and I waited for three months before I went to the Gestapo again. When I was given the permit downstairs I noted that I was allotted only three-quarters of an hour for the interview, whereas for the last two years I had always been granted a full hour. I complained of this to the commissioner, saying that I had a right to an hour.

He replied: "You haven't a right to anything whatever, and if you pay a visit every eight weeks it may very well happen that you'll get no more permits at all." (This was evidently the trouble-maker of whom the secretary had warned me.) I was thankful that I could say: "There must be a misunderstanding. I come here once a quarter; but on the last two occasions I was allowed for special reasons to visit the camp after a two months' interval. Please look in your files; you will see that what I say is correct."

To his evident regret, he had to admit that I was right. But on this visit, and all later occasions, I had to content myself with three-quarters of an hour. He really could not see—he declared—why I couldn't be contented, like everyone else, with a quarter of an hour.

When I rang up the Gestapo three months later Captain H. had left. I was referred to an Assessor Berndorfer, who simply refused to give me a permit.

I appealed to an adjutant of Himmler's, Captain Suchannek, who always saw me when I rang him up, but as a rule only in the lobby; perhaps in order to avoid any more intimate conversation. But it did not prevent me from giving him an exhaustive explanation of my case.

"Captain H.," I told him, "was very glad to know that —without being asked—I had corrected the false reports of my son's case which were current in England; so he gave me his promise that I should visit my son once a quarter. I regard an officer's promise as a word of honour, and since Captain H. is no longer in a position to keep his word of honour I take it as a matter of course that you, in his place, will feel obliged to do so." He thereupon gave me his word that I should visit the camp once a quarter, but warned me against committing the slightest imprudence; for in that case he would have to refuse any further permits.

He sent me to Berndorfer, to whom I was to apply in future. Berndorfer was plainly astonished on receiving Suchannek's orders to give me a permit. He asked me into his room, and engaged me in conversation. He was quite gracious in his manner when he bade me good-day, and I felt that I had somehow found favour in his eyes. My unknown friend, who had warned me against the commissioner, and who happened to be in the room, had apparently formed the same opinion of me, for he kept on giving me approving glances, and he politely escorted me to the door.

From this time onwards I had no more trouble over my permits, which were always given to me by Herr Berndorfer in person.

Directly conditions began to deteriorate I resumed my efforts to influence opinion abroad. I reported every change, taking care that no false rumours should be accepted, but that every alteration for the worse should be realized, and that no one should imagine that things were still as satisfactory as they had been under Reich. This was not easy. I had, of course, to remain absolutely anonymous; it was important that I should continue to seem the loyal and harmless person whom I appeared to the Gestapo. If anything could have been proved against me it would not only have cost me my liberty, but Hans would have been absolutely cut off from the outer world.

Heinz had to make repeated trips abroad, either to Holland or to Prague, from which centres he once more sought to appeal to the conscience of the outer world. This was a dangerous task, but he never dreamed of avoiding danger when his brother's welfare was in question.

Our sympathizers often offered to promote such a widespread agitation as was organized on behalf of Ossietzky. However, we decided that it was better to be circumspect and avoid offensive tactics so long as the situation was endurable. As a matter of course, however, material was provided for articles in the leading foreign newspapers, while prominent and influential persons whose opinion would carry weight in Germany were interested in the case. At a word from us a widespread agitation would have been organized. Preparations were made for any contingency, but it did not seem to us that the proper moment had arrived.

Not until long afterwards did I realize how dangerous these many journeys of Heinz's had been, or learn that on each of his visits to Prague his friends had implored him to remain in Czechoslovakia. They always feared that he would be arrested on his return to Germany. But even had I known these things I should have let him go. We were as though under an obsession: Hans must be helped, no matter what became of us. I was not deterred even by the thought (although in this I was doing violence to myself) that I was leaving all the most dangerous work to Heinz. For it was obvious that I, in Berlin, must attend to the more important work, which no one could do in my place. And it would be worse for Hans if I, and not Heinz, were to be imprisoned.

CHAPTER VI

The Black Courtyard

FOR THREE YEARS and two months Hans was interned in the Lichtenberg camp, living through four different periods under four commandants. It is interesting to note how completely the conditions of life in the camp were dependent on the ruling commandant.

One thing is certain: the higher authorities of the Gestapo and the leaders of the Third Reich never did a thing to ameliorate the deplorable state of affairs prevailing in the camps. The more sadistic a commandant, the more successful his career. I was told again and again that the greatest scoundrels were actually preferred; the more humane officers were regarded as lax and incompetent. The only irreproachable commandant I ever heard of did not keep his post very long; it was felt that he was not sufficiently energetic. Yet he must in actual fact have been a man of great energy, for despite the abominable regulations, for which Himmler was responsible, and which were never modified as long as Hans was in Lichtenburg, he contrived to make the life of the prisoners tolerable, and to enforce discipline among the personnel of the camp, despite the great proportion of criminal types among the guards.

Lichtenberg was a Renaissance building, once the castle of a Saxon princess of the sixteenth century. It became a gaol, and then a convict prison, and now it is surrounded by a wall twelve feet in height, on the top of which is a barbed wire fence, through which runs a high-tension electric current. On arriving at the camp the prisoners' heads are shaved; after this they can allow their hair to grow.

Hans kept his head shaven. A friend of his told me that he preferred a shaven head. In the first place, he found his thick hair uncomfortable, for since the injuries inflicted at Sonnenburg he suffered constantly from pains in the head. In the second place, he had already had his hair torn out by the handful, and while he was close-cropped or shaven this form of torture could not be repeated.

Every prisoner was examined by the doctor on his delivery at the camp. Except in cases of serious illness all were declared "fit." They were lodged in great dormitories under the roof, sixty to a hundred men in each, sleeping in two tiers of army beds, on sacks of straw under woollen blankets. The electric light was kept burning all night. The dormitories were enclosed by a heavy wooden grille, round which the guard patrolled all night. Most of the sentries made as much noise as they could, with the deliberate intention of disturbing the prisoners' sleep.

There was no means of heating the rooms, and many of the prisoners suffered severely from the cold.

Drill or "exercising" constituted the principal activity. With its terrible driving and bullying it was probably much the same in all the camps, varied only by the sadistic inspirations of the company-leader. In Lichtenberg the men were exercised in the "Black Courtyard," known also as "the Death-Circle," because at first the newcomers were driven into this courtyard, where they were made to run round in a circle, encouraged by kicks and blows of the rifle-butt, until several of them fell dead. The bodies were buried in the courtyard. Later on a latrine was established over their graves. An important part of the "exercising" was "crawling." The lifting of the head during this exercise was strictly forbidden. If a man raised his head he was immediately pushed down into the filth and trampled on with nailed boots.

Nothing could ever be done quickly enough. One horrible exercise was rolling in the filth, in a frantic tempo. Many prisoners brought up all that they had in their stomachs. One officer, who had endured the battle of the Somme and all the horrors of the war, and was so severely wounded that he could not take part in the "drill" was seized with vomiting at the mere sight of it, and shaken with sobs like a little child.

Even during the mid-day pause the prisoners were often ordered out for punishment drill—a hundred and fifty knee-bends on the toes, performed in tens. For the old and the invalids a special squad was formed. "Free exercises instead of drill"—but what sort of free exercise? They were often kept at it for five hours without a breathing-space.

One of the special sadistic inventions of the company-leaders was "hopping." Standing erect on the toes of one foot, holding the ankle firmly grasped in the hands, the prisoners had to hop at a given tempo (fifteen hops to the minute) round and round the courtyard, for as long as two hours at a time. If anyone fell behind or needed medical attention afterwards he was a "sneak," who was transferred to a special company, which was harried even worse than the rest.

If anyone can speak of the "drill," the "sports," and the "free exercises" in camp without indignation, let him try them himself at the required tempo!

Here my son's stiff leg was a blessing to him; it dispensed him from this kind of exercise.

The company of homosexuals was treated with especial severity in the Black Courtyard. I spoke to one young man who had recently undergone an operation on the knee. Not the slightest regard was paid to this fact, and he was crippled for life.

This company included a large number of men who were simply regarded as undesirable for political or other reasons; or some personage high in the ranks of the Party had coveted their possessions. Naturally, such men had never been tried or sentenced.

In Lichtenburg, as in all the camps, singing played an important part, and it drove many of the prisoners to desperation. They were tortured by being compelled to sing the most imbecile songs—either Nazi songs or sickly sentimental stuff. An even crueller practice—or so it seemed to me—was to force the prisoners to sing *Wanderlieder*, which celebrated the beauties of Nature and the joys of liberty.

The relieving of the bowels and bladder was a dreadful business. The companies, which had to be under lock and key by a stated time, were taken to the latrines by their guards. The long row of latrines was open, uncovered and unprotected. Here, in the icy cold, in wind and rain, all had to be done in frantic haste, while the guards raved and shouted. Many of the prisoners were unable to relieve themselves for days, because they had been driven off before they had even sat down. Often an *obstipatio neurotica* resulted, which might endanger life.

For meals, and during their leisure, each company was marched into a large separate room, equipped with long tables, wooden benches, electric light, and an iron stove. Many of these rooms had loud-speakers; and here the prisoners had to listen to the speeches of the Führer. They might also listen to music on specified occasions. When the conditions of life in the camp began to deteriorate again Hans wrote in one of his letters: "My only pleasure is the broadcast of the Bach cantatas on Sunday mornings."

Here—as many of his fellow-prisoners told me—Hans would spend his free time as though in another world; absorbed in his studies, despite the noise and confusion.

But the prisoners were seldom left in peace for long. Whenever an SS guard entered the room there was a shout of "Attention!" and all sprang to their feet, standing at attention until the guard gave them the sign to dismiss, or left the room. Many of the guards took a devilish delight in keeping the prisoners standing at attention through the whole of their recreation-time, chatting together without giving the order to dismiss.

A mere perusal of the camp regulations and penalties, displayed on a board and signed "Eicke, Superintendent of the Concentration Camp," told the newcomer that there was no manifestation of life that was not threatened with some penalty.

Every SS man, and indeed every SS recruit, was a superior officer; whatever work he required of the prisoners, whatever order he gave, no matter how senseless, had to be executed. The lightest of the appointed penalties was: five days in a dark cell on a diet of bread and water, with a hot meal on the fourth day. The most trifling infractions of the rules—smoking, for example—were visited with corporal punishment, the lightest being fifteen blows of the stick on the back and buttocks. The highest penalties were: one hundred and fifty blows, solitary confinement, in some cases for several months, and execution by shooting or hanging. The commandant could inflict the death penalty at any time, without legal formalities. No prisoner could move about without an SS guard; he could not even go to the latrine alone. It was the duty of every sentry to shoot any prisoner who approached the wall.

The punishment cells (the "coal-cellars") were in the deeply sunken, cold, absolutely dark cellarage of the west wing of the castle. Each cell contained only a brick platform which served as a bed, and one blanket. Every fourth day the prisoner was given a hot meal, and on the following night a sack of straw. In front of the iron-studded door which shut off the cellars, and behind heavy iron bars, was a space from which a sentry could keep guard over the prisoners. The only article in this space was a bucket for the relief of physical necessities. The prisoners in the cellars—and as a rule the newcomers also—were never under any circumstances provided with toilet-paper, so that anyone who could scrounge a scrap of newspaper hid it away as though it had been a treasure. No prisoner was allowed to wash himself during his term of solitary confinement.

On their discharge all prisoners had to declare in writing that they had been well treated. They were told that if they gave any information "whether true or untrue, as to happenings in the camp" they would be immediately rearrested.

One prisoner, on returning to the world, was greeted

by his friends with the query: "Man, where are your teeth?"

"They were knocked out in Lichtenberg."

No later than the following day he was back in Lichtenberg.

When Hans was transferred to Lichtenberg the camp was in the hands of a fiendish sadist, Commandant Ensberger, known as "the Black." All the prisoners spoke of him with hatred and abhorrence. Fortunately he left soon after my son's arrival; indeed, Hans escaped his attentions, for he had to spend some days in the infirmary, as his leg was not improved by the journey to the camp which took nearly a week. Ensberger had allowed many prisoners to be tortured to death. Each week several coffins were made in the carpenter's shop. It was always known for whom they were intended.

Only in one case (a prisoner told me) was it impossible to find out the name of the intended occupant. But I was able to tell him the name, for this man cost Ensberger his post as commandant.

Ensberger, like so many of the SS, was on very bad terms with the SA. On the 30th June, 1934, a number of SA men were delivered at Lichtenberg, "merely as a temporary measure of precaution." Among them was a troop-leader[1] of the SA. A week later he was dead.

---

[1] A *Standartenführer* of stormtroopers: the *Standart* is equivalent to a regiment. so the *Standartenführer* would be, in our terminology, colonel or C.O. of a party regiment.—Tr.

Ensberger himself had killed him, slowly and brutally.

Since the man was a *Standartenführer*, Ensberger was removed from his post. The prisoners even cherished hopes that he had been packed off to a concentration camp, or sentenced to a term of imprisonment in a convict prison.

Ensberger was followed by Commandant Schmidt. What the prisoners had to suffer under him is shown by two descriptions which I received from eye-witnesses. Each of these came from the pen of an educated man, and I am sure that they contain exact observations and are not exaggerated, for I have heard the same sort of account over and over again.

A prisoner, a man of about fifty, who had been promoted officer during the war in recognition of valour in the field, and who had been awarded the Iron Cross, first class, and the gold armlet, which was given only to men who had been wounded at least five times, had already received 25 blows in Columbia House on account of "contempt of the SS." This man was now called out and informed that for the same offence, for which he had already been punished in Columbia House, he would now receive fifteen blows and sixteen days' confinement in a dark cell, etc. In the morning, when we were washing, I saw the man's back was still covered with black and blue weals from his former maltreatment.

A wooden stool and four sticks were brought and placed in the middle of the courtyard. The man tried to explain that he had already been punished for this offence.

No one listened to him. SS men dragged him to the stool, and one of them, seizing him by the neck, forced him down. He lay down on the stool. He was rather tall, and it was some time before he was lying in the right position. His knees were touching the ground. Two SS men kicked him repeatedly in the hollow of the knees in order to make him crawl closer to the stool. At last he was in the correct position. Two SS men took up their stand on either side of the stool. Each had a stick about forty inches long in his hand. Behind them stood Herr Fettke, Herr Schmidt, and all the company-leaders and SS under-officers.

Commandant Schmidt gave the order: "Begin!" At first the men brandished their sticks a few times, so that one heard them whistling through the air. Then they raised them high above their heads. Each leaned back as far as he could, and swung his stick back in readiness, and only then came the first swishing blow, immediately followed by the second. The man did not utter a sound. Again the two fellows swung back their sticks, and again two blows came swishing down on the victim. The tortured man clenched his teeth. The camp commandant roared: "The fellow isn't feeling anything!"

A third time the two blows fell on him. Still the prisoner was silent. The commandant began to rave. "Still stubborn, are you, you dog! Two others have a try!" The two "reserve strikers" came forward. Each whirled his stick through the air; then both struck the prisoner, swinging the stick far back before the blow.

Eight blows—ten—twelve. The prisoner bore his punishment like a hero. Not a sound escaped between his teeth. Now Camp-leader Fettke and Company-leader

Bräunig seized a stick apiece, and struck the last three blows. One of them struck one blow the other two, but they were both crimson in the face from the effort! The prisoner bore everything, to the last blow, without a sound. The commandant and the SS leaders were foaming with rage. They felt that they were scorned by the man, that their honour was insulted. But—alas!—the punishment had been awarded.

The victim was ordered to stand up. With difficulty he lifted himself to his feet. He looked like a dying man. Then he had to pick up the stool and the sticks, and the jailers of the cellars took him away to serve his sixteen days' solitary confinement.

Laden with the stool and the sticks, the man had to cross the courtyard between the companies of the prisoners, who were standing breathless at attention. There he was told to "Halt!"—and Herr Schmidt made a little speech, in which he explained that only a light punishment had been awarded that day; but he promised his hearers that the next offender would not be let off so lightly.

The most horrifying thrashing which I ever saw inflicted while I was in Lichtenburg was something so terrible that it ought to be described in detail.

On a Sunday in March, about five o'clock in the afternoon, the alarm sirens of the camp suddenly began to howl. In such a case all the prisoners were ordered, no matter where they might be, to go immediately to the "day-rooms" and form into companies.

My company had just been taken out to go to the latrines. Immediately the SS men bellowed: "Right about turn! Into the hall!" Although we had a few one-legged war-cripples with us we managed to reach the stairs before the SS men billeted on the first story of the building could leave their rooms. Just as we were passing the doors of these rooms the SS men came rushing down the stairs in their steel helmets, carrying their rifles, and running down all who were in their way. The sirens were still howling. A few minutes later the company-leader appeared with a larger body of SS men, and called the roll. Then he left us standing. We stood until about seven o'clock, and were then suddenly sent to bed without supper.

Next day all was as usual in the camp. The prisoners had no idea at first what all the excitement of the day before had been about, nor why the guards had been strengthened. Very gradually the news trickled through that on the Sunday afternoon three prisoners from the so-called "Professional Criminals' Company" had broken out of camp and had disappeared.

I learned by chance how the escape had been effected. The three men had heard that the "habitual criminals" (how far the men of this company were actually habitual criminals I cannot say) were to be transferred, in a few days' time, to the most dreadful of all the concentration camps—Papenburg-Esterwegen. Such alarming reports of this camp were current that the three men resolved to escape this fate by flight.

In the whole of the camp there was only one window which was not barred. This was on the second floor of the hospital building. It overlooked the street. With the help of torn sheets the three men contrived to escape. A later report said they had been employed as bricklayers in the cellars, and had broken a hole in the wall, through which they escaped.

The commandant was in a terribly excited state. Neither the thirteen-foot wall, nor the electrically charged barbed wire fence, nor the sentries watching over the gates, nor the host of SS guards, had been of avail.

On Tuesday the prisoners heard that one of the fugitives had been caught. On Wednesday it was rumoured that all three were back in camp, and were now in the cellars.

On Thursday the roll was called at dinner-time. All the companies were already drawn up. Some prisoners dragged a table to the middle of the courtyard. It was seven feet long. Suddenly the three prisoners appeared in the entry leading from the first courtyard. They were laden with cords and sticks, and surrounded by a number of SS men.

These were the fugitives. Two were elderly men; the third a pale, tall young fellow in the early twenties. They all looked terrible. Pale as death, their faces smeared with blood, they crept across the courtyard. The younger man walked more than ten paces behind the others. He could hardly move. The three men must have been terribly maltreated. Their linen prison clothes—even in the hardest winter this company had only old drill suits— were torn. It made me shudder to look at these men. Their aspect spoke for itself: it told me how terrible their flight must have been, how frightful their recapture, how horrible their treatment when caught.

The three men stood facing the table and waited. All felt that something ghastly was going to happen. What, no one knew. After Herr Fettke had called the roll of the companies there was again an oppressive silence in the courtyard. At last, after a pause of some ten minutes, the commandant, Herr Obersturmbannführer Schmidt, appeared, with a large retinue. He accepted the roll. We expected that Herr Fettke would now read the "sentence." But this was not what happened.

His face red as a lobster, Herr Schmidt stepped out into the middle of the court, where he made the following speech:

"You know that three persons in protective confinement have attempted to break away. We have caught the curs again. It is God's pity (God's pity! he said) that they were not shot on the run. But I have means of making up for that!" And Herr Schmidt turned round to his SS men and made a sign with his hand. The SS men flung themselves on one of the prisoners—one of the elder men. Ten of the fellows seized him and threw him on the table. In his deadly terror the man struggled and tried to defend himself, but they seized him and held him fast. The cords were uncoiled, and the man was bound fast upon the table.

Then the camp commandant roared: "And now you are going to get something! This is what happens to everyone who tries to escape from the camp!—Go at it!"

This time there were not two but four men who struck simultaneously. The blows were not numbered—but some of the prisoners counted them. The man endured the first twenty blows in silence. Then he began to scream. But the raving voice of the commandant shouted him down.

"Strike harder!" he bellowed. "The fellow's not feeling it!"

And the SS men struck. For a time the man continued to whimper; then he must have lost consciousness. For the space of some twenty or thirty blows we thought he was already dead, but then he began to shriek again. The SS men worked themselves up into a paroxysm. They tore the sticks out of one another's hands, shouting, "Let's just have a smack at him!" At last Herr Schmidt shouted "Stop!" But his SS men did not hear him. He had to shout a second time and a third time before the hounds left their prey.

When at last the cords were loosened the tortured man fell from the table. But the commandant shouted: "No play-acting here! Next man!"

The SS men seized the other elderly man and flung him on the table. While he was being bound others dragged the first man on to the grass and left him lying there.

The prisoners, looking on at this horrid spectacle, had been fairly calm at first. But when it seemed as though the blows were never going to cease some of them began to murmur. The SS men paid no attention to them. In one company two epileptics had seizures, while others began to vomit.

Meanwhile the second victim was tied fast, and Schmidt gave the sign to begin. The man struggled as he lay on the table. Again and again the cords with which he was bound had to be drawn tighter.

But his struggling had utterly infuriated Herr Schmidt and his gang. They flogged away like men threshing corn. They wrested the sticks from one another's hands. They had worked themselves into a paroxysm over the first man; now they were in a frenzy. Each blow was like the effort of a professional strong man who knows that admiring eyes are watching him. The prisoners began to rage. Men who at other times were too fearful to open their mouths began to shout: "You curs! You murderers! You criminals!" But nothing could check the SS men and their master. From time to time a prisoner lying in convulsions was carried off behind the ranks to the infirmary. Herr Schmidt and his brutes were busied with more interesting matters.

For a long time the prisoner lay completely unconscious. He felt nothing more, but the threshers went on threshing. At last he too was relinquished. Herr Schmidt had him untied. Looking distractedly about him, the poor man stood before the table, on which the third, younger man had been thrown and bound. This man bit and struck out at his torturers, defending himself like a madman, with almost incredible strength. Again and again he shook off his assailants, but at last he too was overcome.

By this time the SS men were reeling in a sort of ecstasy. They no longer saw where their blows were falling; they simply struck, and bellowed at every blow. Above the uproar one heard the shrill screams of the victim. The other two had not shrieked a great deal; the third man screamed horribly. He was fully conscious all the time; no merciful swoon engulfed him. He bled until the blood ran over the table and dripped over the edges on to the ground. Everything suddenly turned blue before my eyes. Some of the men in my company seized me under the arms and held me up. I had to force myself not to vomit; I felt the tears running down my face. I watched a mob of devils leaping about and raving.

They were roaring as though they were paid for it. And suddenly it was all over.

The man was untied. Herr Schmidt rubbed his hands and shouted: "That's what happens to anyone who tries to make a bunk! Just you mark that!"

As in a dream I saw the then dying men drag the heavy table, on which lay the cords, across the courtyard. Even this was not spared the unhappy men. Dripping with blood, they no longer looked human. I learned afterwards that the first man had received 186 blows, the second 175, and the last about 150.

Next morning it was known in the camp that one of the three had died in the night. Another had hanged himself in his cell. Of the third I never heard again.

On the following day there was no drill and no duty. The SS men were all busied with the transfer of the penal company to Papenburg-Esterwegen. From a window I saw them, surrounded by a strong cordon of SS men, being herded to the railway station. And I could only think: "God have mercy on your souls!"

During the following week the supreme head of the SS, Himmler himself, came to inspect the camp. And shortly after this Herr Schmidt was removed from his post. Many prisoners believed that he would have to pay for his inhumanity. It was said that his predecessor had been sentenced to eight years' imprisonment on a charge of murder and maltreatment of prisoners. But Herr Schmidt got off more lightly. It is true that he left the camp so that it should be made clear that the supreme authorities did not approve of such terrible manhandling, but he left Lichtenberg only to take up a similar command in another camp.

These incidents show that the Nazi leaders (Hitler, Himmler, Göring, and others) have full knowledge of the crimes committed in the concentration camps. But they interfere only when some particular case excites too much comment. They tolerate the prevailing state of affairs, but they do not like it to be made public. Where crime is punished, as in Ensberger's case, it is because the crime has been committed against a Nazi. In other cases —as in that of Schmidt—there was a mere pretence of punishment; actually the offender was merely transferred and often actually promoted.

I knew that Hans had not suffered any such maltreatment as is here described during his internment in Lichtenburg (for except in the beginning, as to which I could never obtain anything but vague rumours, nothing particularly horrible seems to have happened to him). But the prisoners had to witness these punishments. All spoke of this only with the utmost horror. How dreadful it must have seemed to one who ate no meat, saying: "How could I ever kill an animal to benefit myself?"— who at the age of two used to go into the garden after rain, to collect the earthworms and carry them into the shrubbery, because he had noticed that after rain the worms used to crawl across the paths, where they were crushed by heedless feet! He whispered once, when I had succeeded in asking how he had been treated: "I am not ill-treated; but the things I have to witness!"

No prisoner of my acquaintance ever spoke of having suffered such punishments. One, whom I knew very well, did once bring himself, at my request, to speak plainly. I knew, from my son's hints, that something dreadful had been done to him, and I knew also that Hans had been terribly disturbed for months on end, because he was afraid "that they meant to finish" his friend. The man described such a scene as that recorded above. He spoke in a curiously calm, absent-minded fashion, as though the matter did not really concern him; quietly and dispassionately. I was impressed; I thought: "Has the man really got over all this, that he can speak of it so calmly?" I asked him, almost timidly: "You will never forget that?" He replied, very calmly and quietly: "No." He looked in my eyes for a moment, but this brief moment betrayed the same unsubduable longing for vengeance, the same fanatical hatred which I felt myself. How often have I seen this look in the eyes of prisoners when they have spoken of their torturers!

I knew that none of them would be absent when the day of retribution arrived.

PART III

BUCHENWALD AND DACHAU

CHAPTER I

Uta of Naumburg

CONDITIONS IN LICHTENBERG had visibly deteriorated. I knew that for Hans too the good times were over. Nevertheless, after all the terrible things which he had experienced in the past, and after the reports of atrocities which we had received from some of the other camps, it seemed to me that the state of affairs was still endurable.

Then something happened which caused me terrible misgivings.

Dr. Berndorfer, whom I had rung up at the end of July 1937, saying that I was about to call for my visitor's permit, which was then due, apologized profoundly when I entered his office. He had just realized that my son was in Lichtenberg. That being so, he regretted that he could give me no permit; all visits to Lichtenberg were prohibited; he was terribly sorry that he had sent for me unnecessarily.

I was so shocked by this that a big tear ran down my cheek; a thing which had never happened to me before in the offices of the Gestapo. As Dr. Berndorfer was looking at me with a highly embarrassed and compassionate expression, I deliberately let myself go; I began to cry, saying: "Excuse me for losing control of myself like this, but the prohibition of a visit is almost always connected with terrible happenings in the camp!"

He swore that the reason for the prohibition was purely technical. But I insisted that there must be some other reason. My tears apparently softened him, for he said: "Well, I mustn't really tell you what the reason is. But it distresses me that you should feel such needless anxiety. You must promise me not to tell a living soul. The Lichtenberg camp is being broken up. The prisoners are being sent elsewhere, not far from Weimar, and in the midst of all the confusion which such a move involves it is naturally impossible to allow visitors."

To hear this was of course a great relief to me, and when Dr. Berndorfer once more apologized for my fruitless errand, I said: "I am very grateful to you for your failure of memory; I am sure I never should have got the real truth out of you at the telephone"; which he smilingly admitted.

Soon after this we had a letter from Hans. He was at Buchenwald. The letter was signed "Hans" instead of the usual "Hans Achim." This meant "I am being maltreated."

I immediately rang up Dr. Berndorfer. "Now that my son is in the new camp," I said, "I suppose I can go to see him."

No, I must have patience for a time. I could not go so soon after the removal. He would let me know when I could have a permit.

The next letter was very short; it said nothing at all, and the handwriting was dreadful. Again it was signed "Hans."

Heinz had got into touch with certain people whose political sympathies were leftward; for this was the only way of obtaining prompt information as to changes in the camp. These people were mostly relatives of prisoners interned in the same camp as Hans. It was possible in this way to compare reports and to integrate them.

Another prisoner, who had hitherto made no complaint, wrote a very disturbing letter to his wife. This woman—a simple-minded creature—did not dare to take any steps on her own account, so when I next asked to see Dr. Berndorfer I referred to a conversation which I had had with her. I told him that the wife of a prisoner had called on me and had informed me that she had reliable information that in Buchenwald there was a dreadful state of affairs, and that I ought to do something about it with the help of the Gestapo. Moreover, my son's last letter had caused me terrible anxiety.

Dr. Berndorfer tried to reassure me again. Of course things were not very comfortable while a camp was being organized. Perhaps there weren't enough blankets; possibly some of the prisoners had been cold at night; but that would soon be put right.

I replied that I was far from being so optimistic. I had a very acute intuition of the sort of thing that happened in camp, and I begged him, very urgently, to make inquiries.

"I am afraid, for example, that in the work of organizing the camp no attention will be paid to my son's bad state of health, and his crippled leg." And I begged him to see for himself what a condition my son was in, and to make sure that he was decently treated.

"I will," he said, "when opportunity offers." I retorted vehemently: "I don't like the word 'offers'; in plain German it means 'never.' I am not going to leave this room until I have your firm promise that you will do something at once on my son's behalf!" He gave the required promise; but I could see that he was wavering between his compassion for me and his dread of the camp commandant.

As the next letter from Hans again made a very bad impression on me I rang up the Gestapo once more, asked for a visitor's permit, and inquired whether Dr. Berndorfer had done anything.

Yes, he assured me; everything was in capital order, and my son was going on very well. I am convinced, however, that he had not dared to make any inquiries at the camp. I had the impression that this man was quite good-hearted, and that he would willingly have helped me, but that he had no influence whatever, and was in deadly fear of endangering his position if he should put himself forward in any way. The days in which the official in charge of the camps could run the risk of giving an order to a camp commandant were apparently long past.

One of the prisoners had repeatedly spoken, in one of his letters, of the beautiful wood in which they were living, so that his relatives declared: "That must have some meaning." It struck us that he might be trying to say: "Just have a look at this wood; it isn't yet fenced off."

And I thought at once: Perhaps while the camp is still being organized, before it is completely fenced off, it would be possible to attempt a rescue. At all events, the "beautiful wood" must be examined.

I went to Weimar and called on an acquaintance, a thoroughly good fellow. He, too, agreed that the matter must be looked into. We decided over the week-end to organize a regular scouting party from Weimar. Heinz and I would take part in it. Two cars were placed at our disposal. We meant to stroll through the wood, in order to determine just where the camp was situated. We intended also to question the inhabitants of the adjacent villages. The women would get themselves up like Sunday excursionists, while the men would try to make people talk in the local taverns. I planned also to call on a few reliable pastors.

For a long while, of course, I had been telling the outer world that the most terrible conditions were prevailing in Buchenwald. I was especially anxious to arouse the interest of the Christian world; but before I could do this I must ascertain whether any prisoners were interned in Buchenwald on religious grounds. And this I hoped to learn from the pastors of the neighbourhood.

A woman friend of mine, who knew something of politics and with whom I discussed this scheme, as indeed I discussed all that I was doing, was utterly opposed to my plan of taking part in the expedition. She assured me that all motor-cars would be repeatedly held up on the roads, when the passengers and any baggage they might have would be narrowly inspected. If I, Frau Litten, were found in a motor-car in the neighbourhood of Buchenwald I should certainly have a most unpleasant time. I laughed at her, but she was terribly distressed, and at last, bursting into tears, she begged me for her sake to abandon the plan; so I gave in to her, and I also forbade Heinz to join the party.

She was quite right. The reconnaissance was a pitiful failure. Two parties of motorists, one consisting of an elderly gentleman with two daughters, and the other of a mother with her son, parked their cars by the edge of the wood, which they then explored. They had gone barely a hundred yards when they were halted by SS men and taken to the nearest police station. Their assurances that they had merely left their cars to go for a stroll in the wood were unavailing. They had to give their names and addresses, and they were kept in custody for two days while these were being verified. As nothing could be proved against them they were released, but for a long while they were kept under observation.

No one had succeeded in penetrating the wood. The only result of this excursion was the discovery that the people of the neighbourhood were completely intimidated; they did not dare to give any detailed information. They had been warned that they were to know nothing of the erection of the camp. If they said anything about it they would be imprisoned.

A card dated 17th October, 1937, said: "My address is Dachau." Again the signature was "Hans," not "Hans Achim."

A fellow-prisoner who had been discharged from Lichtenburg informed me that if Hans ever wrote anything about Uta of Naumburg he would always be referring to himself.

At the end of September Hans had written in a letter from Buchenwald: "Part of the literary supplement of an old issue of the *Völkischer Beobachter* came into my hands here, in which there was a review of several books that have lately appeared on the German culture of the Middle Ages. I gather from this that according to recent researches the Margravine Uta of Naumburg, after her separation from Burkard, was imprisoned first in a convent not far from her ancestral castle, and later in a

Bavarian convent, where she is said to have died. I cannot give the title and publisher of this book, as the beginning of the review was torn out."

It was clear that Burkard (von Hohenfels), the name of an actual Minnesinger, was the name given to the friend who had been in Lichtenburg with Hans. The convent in the neighbourhood of their ancestral castle (Lichtenburg) was Buchenwald, and the Bavarian convent was Dachau. Following closely upon this came a letter from the new address, Dachau.

I applied immediately for a visitor's permit on the grounds that Dachau was a long-established camp in which everything would be in order. Dr. Berndorfer promised me that I should receive a permit, but not just yet.

I wrote to Hans that the book which he had mentioned (which, of course, had never existed) was a historical novel, to which the experts attached no value whatever, as it was mainly a work of imagination. There was an Anglo-Saxon manuscript which stated definitely that Uta had very soon left the convent, had rejoined Burkard, and had lived a happy and normal life far from her ancestral castle. This was to give him courage; and the mention of the Anglo-Saxon manuscript—highly improbable, of course, in connection with the history of Uta of Naumburg—was to tell him that there were people working for him in England, who believed that he would soon be set free.

As a matter of fact, Lord Allen was once more doing what he could for Hans; and he appealed to the German Embassy in London for an improvement in the prisoner's now deplorable situation.

In his next letter Hans asked me to discover the authorship of the ballad which describes how Alkuin von Hartwald took the convent by storm in order to liberate Uta; but he had delayed too long, and found only her corpse, for she had hanged herself in her nun's veil. This was plain speaking. From his first remark we were convinced that he had been told, in Buchenwald, and again in Dachau, that he must make an end of himself within the next three months, or they would save him the trouble. We knew all about this procedure, which had been applied in the case of Mühsam.

It was plain that this letter was an appeal for help. But what was the significance of Alkuin von Hartwald? It often happened that Hans would mention a name which was unknown to us. We accordingly made a practice of carefully investigating any name which was unfamiliar. If it could not be found in the reference books it was evidently a camouflage.

We knew the Anglo-Saxon Alcuin, but we could discover no such person as an Alkuin von Hartwald, or indeed a Hartwald of any kind. We pondered and searched; and suddenly the scales fell from Heinz's eyes. Alkuin and Allen had the same initial and final letters. And Hartwald was simply a translation of Hurtwood. Hans knew from my allusions that English friends were once more planning to agitate for his release. What he really meant was simply: "If Lord Allen does not make haste I shall be dead."

I sent this information to England, begging our friends to take prompt and energetic action. Hans must hope for the best and try to hold out. I wrote to him saying that I could not discover the ballad of which he spoke. There must be some mistake; probably he had confused it with Dahn's "Mette von Marienburg," in which "the valiant Swabian Stauf," at the moment of greatest peril, rescues the knight from certain death. My children had often called me, in jest, "the valiant Swabian Stauf." He would understand from this that I was doing my very utmost on his behalf.

CHAPTER II

I Denounce a "Traitor"

ONE DAY A DETECTIVE called on me, showed me some
photographs of Hans, and asked, "Who is that?" I replied immediately: "That is my son." To his further
questions I gave him all the particulars of Hans' life.
He was about to leave the room, saying, "Thank you,
that's all right!" when I detained him. "Will you allow
me to ask a question now? What does all this mean?"

"Oh, it's the usual thing," he said. "Every criminal
who is delivered into custody is photographed, and we
show the photographs to his relatives in order to verify
his identity; for it very often happens that criminals go
about under false names with false papers, and that later
on some perfectly innocent man has to suffer for their
misuse of them. If we check the details with the man's
relatives we have proof that they are genuine."

"You have just used the word 'criminal,'" I objected.
"I must really ask you to take that back. You don't appear to know that you are speaking of a political internee,
and I can't imagine that you regard a political internee
as a criminal!"

He flushed deeply. "No, of course I didn't mean that. I only meant that criminals often do as I've said, so that we have to go through this procedure in the case of every prisoner."

"Would you be so kind," I said, "as to show me my son's portrait again?" He showed me the sheet, but he covered the lower part of the photographs with both hands. One of the photographs was in profile; it was a definitely intellectual head; in the other two, which were full-face, the eyes were completely distracted.

"What are you covering with your hands?" I asked.

"Oh, you are not supposed to know where your son is."

"But I know that he's in Dachau."

"Well, then, we needn't make a secret of it!" Under the pictures was the superscription: "Hans Litten. Dachau." But he still covered one part of the sheet, saying: "That you definitely must not see. That's the prisoner's number."

Of course, I managed to get a squint under his hand, and I read the number: 3000 and something. So the camp has at least three thousand prisoners!

My son's photograph, together with his last letter, disturbed me dreadfully. I was still more distressed by a visit which I received the following day.

When I opened the door in response to a ring a man forced his way in and closed the door behind him. Then, speaking quietly but imperatively, he said: "Sixth block, third room. What's that?"

"That," I said, "is my son's address in Dachau."

"Good; then I know you are Hans Litten's mother."

Then, still quietly, but very urgently: "Your son," he said, "is being driven to suicide, systematically, purposely, by brutal maltreatment. Do what you can to help him!"

"Who are you? Have you come from my son?"

"No, I don't know your son. I have never been a prisoner. I come from quite another circle."

"Won't you tell me more?"

"No, I should be in danger."

"I'll go to the Gestapo. But what am I to say?"

"The truth!" he said, suddenly speaking quite loudly. He opened the door and was off.

I wrote down the whole conversation. Then I asked Heinz, over the telephone, to come home. We decided that the only reasonable course was to tell the Gestapo just what had happened, and to ask for drastic action in Dachau.

I begged Captain Suchannek urgently for an interview, and he received me at once. I told him just what had happened during the last few days, and also spoke of the bad impression which my son's last few letters had produced. I mentioned also the visit of an English-woman who was passing through Berlin; she had told me in great indignation of the rumours current about Buchenwald, declaring that with the best will in the world there could never be any understanding with Germany as long as one heard of such things.

"Of course," replied Suchannek, "we know very well that there's another atrocity campaign on abroad. And we know why. [At that time the discussion as to the restoration of the German colonies was attracting much attention.] But we didn't know that they were bringing your son in again."

"This isn't a question of an atrocity campaign; it's a question of facts. There's a terrible state of things in Dachau. You must stop it."

"Don't let people persuade you of such things."

"I allow no one to persuade me of anything. Not even you. If everything were in order in Dachau you could allow me to see my son. Why am I not given a visitor's permit? There's a reason for that. There is something which has to be hidden from me."

He seemed embarrassed, yet there was a threat in his voice. "What you tell me is so serious that it will have to be told to the Reichsführer [Himmler]."

"I too consider that to be urgently necessary. But I ask you to allow me to tell these things to Himmler myself. I think they would make more impression on him than if you were to tell them."

He disappeared. He returned about half an hour later. To my regret, he did not take me to Himmler; he merely said: "You will receive a visitor's permit during the next few days, in order that you may convince yourself that all is well with your son. However, what you have told me is so serious that I must ask you to repeat it, just as you have told it to me, to the Criminal Commissioner, Herr Heller."

So I told my story again to Herr Heller. "How can you believe such nonsense!" he said. "Such things don't happen!"

"But such things have already happened!" I insisted. "That is absolutely proven; so they can happen again."

"Oh, you are thinking of Sonnenburg. We have already discussed that affair, and I went there myself with Dr. S. You know that we put a stop to it immediately. Such things won't happen again."

"If you really believe that," I retorted, "you are very badly informed. Such things went on happening constantly. Then there was a short intermission, at least as far as my son was concerned, and now all the horrors are happening again. You can place absolute reliance on what I am saying."

I told him of some of the ghastly things which my son had already endured. And of my interview with the commandant of Brandenburg, and his exclamation: "The prisoners shall pay for this!"

"That," he said, "was really a very stupid thing to say."

"Stupid, you call it! I should use quite another term for such behaviour. And the difference between our judgments of such an exclamation explains the difference of our attitude to what has been happening!"

At last he said: "I understand; you will have to see

for yourself what things are like in Dachau. However, what you have told me is so serious that I must ask you to make a deposition."

A secretary was sent for. Heller briefly explained what was required, and took me into a larger room, where some six people were working at separate tables.

I was expected then and there to dictate my deposition to a shorthand-writer. I began to realize what these people wanted of me. As for me, I was anxious to gain a little time. So I assumed the part which I had so often played with success: that of a talkative but not very intelligent old lady. "What, you mean I just have to dictate what I said? Well, but however shall I put it? You must help me, you know!"

The secretary did help me, very amiably, and only then was the story placed on record for the criminal commissioner.

I was very incompetent. I let him, without protest, word the whole thing himself. But nothing was said to explain why this encounter was of such importance to me. The fact that I found my son looking dreadfully ill seemed to him quite unimportant; but I insisted. "No, that is precisely the essential thing; that is why I have come forward with this information."

"Very well, then, we'll write: 'I thought that my son did not look very well.'"

What could I do then but abandon my diffident rôle? "That won't do," I said. "After all, I have to sign the document when it is written. So write this: 'My son's expression was so dreadful that I knew he had been seriously maltreated.' "

Now came the difficult point. I was expected to give information concerning my English connections. Here I really had to manipulate the facts a little. The English lady who had called on me was a stranger. She had told me her name, of course, but I had not taken it in, and I was too polite to ask her to repeat it. "You know," I said, "English people are always so difficult to understand. Perhaps you yourself know English so well that you wouldn't find them so; unfortunately, I don't."

"What did you talk about?" He was interested in this story of the English lady. "Did she speak German well?"

"I think my English was better than her German. But we were perfectly agreed upon one point—we could understand each other well enough for that—namely, that what has been done to my son must profoundly shock any decent human being. The lady declared that any Englishman who had been in favour of an understanding with Germany would feel, when he heard of it, that no understanding with such a people was possible."

Now they were very anxious to know who this Englishwoman could be. The other occupants of the room, who had long ago laid aside their pens in order to listen to my examination, were very keen to guess. First of all I must describe her appearance. As the lady was small and elegant, I described her as tall, rather lanky, and very much the sportswoman. Yes, she looked just what one expects the average Englishwoman to look.

What would her profession have been? I hadn't, of course, a notion. But she was a cultured and energetic woman, evidently a very influential person, and certainly an active political worker; otherwise she would not have been so interested in such matters.

They repeated a number of English names, some of which were quite familiar to me. They also mentioned a woman to whom I had spoken a few days earlier, and assured me, quite frankly, that she had called on them some time before in connection with the welfare of the internees. My description fitted one of the women whom they had mentioned fairly well; but fortunately one of the clerks observed that she had spoken German fluently. No, this woman could not be the mysterious visitor, for she had interjected only an occasional word of German.

Now I came to the third and most important visit.

"Here," I said, "I don't need your help. The matter was so important that the moment my visitor had left me I wrote an exact record of our conversation. I will dictate it to you."

I described the incident as vividly and dramatically as possible, and dictated my record of our conversation, and as I concluded with my visitor's final words, "The truth!" "And the man was gone!" the secretary sprang to his feet.

"Most extraordinary!" he cried, and the clerk echoed him: "Most extraordinary!"

"Very well, Frau Litten, all we need now is the description of this man."

"I don't quite understand what you mean."

"Well, of course, we must know exactly what the man looks like."

"I came here to make a complaint. You are asking me to denounce somebody. I shall not describe this man."

"You are going to describe this man!" There was a certain menace in the statement.

"He came to me in order to help my son, and I am now to describe him and deliver him into your hands! If I do such a thing as that I am a most abominable woman." [1]

"If you do it," said the secretary, in emphatic tones, "you are a good German."

"No," I cried indignantly, "it's beyond me to understand how one can be a good German and a most abominable woman. I am not going to denounce the man!"

Very quietly the secretary said: "You must describe the man."

There was a pause. I reflected. It was obvious that I should have to denounce the man. All these people were keenly interested in my efforts; they were sympa-

____
[1] Literally "a very great swine."—Tr.

thetic. I could not afford to spoil everything. I had learned often enough, in my dealings with the Gestapo, how important was the good will of each individual, even of the most subordinate employee, and what obstacles they could put in my way if I offended them. The thought was never far from their minds: "Perhaps this fine lady needs taking down a peg: we'll just show her that we've got the upper hand of her!" I knew how annoyed such people had often been if I had simply gone over their heads and had obtained what I wanted from some higher official, whom I was careful to approach as a woman of the world. Here, then, I must try to retain their sympathies, and I must do it so effectually that they would suppress their instinctive longing to show that they had the whip hand of the "lady." Moreover, if I came here merely to make a vehement complaint of the brutal treatment of prisoners I was simply an enemy of the State. I must therefore go warily, and denounce the traitor. If I did not do so I certainly should not receive a visitor's permit, and I should never again be treated so considerately as in the past. On the other hand, if I denounced my visitor I should be behaving in the spineless manner only too common nowadays; in short, as people usually behaved in the offices of the Gestapo. And of one thing I was perfectly sure—that my uncompromising attitude had often made an impression on these people, and that in the last resort it was only through this attitude that I had ever achieved anything.

It was very difficult to come to a decision. The people were all staring at me excitedly, and when the secretary spoke again his voice was urgent.

"Now, Frau Litten, if you please!"

I sprang to my feet, paced excitedly to and fro, and made it clear that I was wrestling with myself. "No," I cried, "I can't bring myself to denounce the man!"

"Frau Litten, you will describe him!"

I drew a deep breath; then at last I said: "Very well, I'll denounce him. After all, the man who called on me told me to tell the truth. Perhaps he foresaw what you would ask me to do, and meant by this remark that I was not to consider him. Well, ask what you want to know!"

I described "a tall, slender, handsome, powerful-looking man."

"Hair?"

"Fair."

"Eyes?"

"Oh, what was their colour? They were bright, almost glittering, and they seemed to look right through me; yes, they must have been blue."

"What would you think his profession would be?"

"It's difficult to say. The criminal commissioner had been to see me the day before; and at first I thought he was more or less in the same position. But his bearing was so authoritative that I felt that he must be someone more important. When he came in I thought: This is someone from the Gestapo. For example, he could have been a *Standartenführer* in civilian clothes. In the old days I should have assumed that he was an officer in mufti. On the other hand, he had such a definitely intellectual head that if I had seen only his head I should have taken him to be an intellectual of some sort."

"What would be your estimate of his height?"

"Well, he was tall."

"No, no, I mean in centimetres. Was he 160 centimetres, or 165?"

"That I can't tell you. I don't think of a person's height in centimetres. For example, I've no idea what my own height is in centimetres."

He stood up and asked, with a rather fatuous smile: "Was he as tall as I am?"

I stood beside him for comparison. "Oh, no, much taller. You see, I had to look right up at him."

"Well, then, we'll say . . ." and he named some figure which I have forgotten.

"And now for his clothes!"

"Well, then I must honestly confess that I haven't the least idea. When he came in my first thought was: 'Good heavens, what a magnificent head!' I really didn't notice anything else."

"What sort of a hat was he wearing?"

"Hat? I can't remember. No, he can't have been wearing a hat. I noticed his fair, glossy hair. Possibly he was carrying his hat in his hand. But I can't say."

"And what sort of a suit was he wearing?"

"That I don't know." Thoughtfully: "He had a cloak, and I think it was open."

"What sort of a cloak? A smart-looking garment, or a cheap, ready-made affair!"

I replied very innocently: "Well, you know, I would really rather not say. Suppose you find the man; and suppose he is wearing a very smart coak, or a very shabby one. If I have described it wrongly you will think I am untrustworthy, or you may even punish me. You see, it's such a frightfully personal matter. I know people who wear the most expensive clothes and yet look shabby, and I know people who look magnificent in the shabbiest garments. For example, I remember saying to the young officers who used to frequent our house, when I saw them in mufti: 'The dickens only knows how you boys always manage to look so nice, for I'm sure you got that suit at a jumble sale!'"

My audience smiled. I could read in their eyes what they were thinking: "Amusing old lady!—a cross-examination of this sort is rather fun!"

However, I was urgently requested to say whether this much-discussed cloak was self-coloured or had a herring-bone pattern. I did not know. But apparently this detail was essential; the document would not be complete without it. So at last I said: "Then I will decide on a herring-bone pattern. But I am really doing so at random. Perhaps you will make a note to that effect in the deposition. I shouldn't wish my credibility to be questioned over a point of that sort."

Again my questioner glanced at his subordinates with a smile. "Touching that she should be so concerned about such a detail. But a woman who is so cautious in her statements must surely be a reliable witness!"

None of my hearers seemed to suspect that my description was absolutely false and misleading.

Now it was the turn of the detective, whose description they had forgotten to take down. "Do you know," I said, "I positively cannot tell you anything very definite. The man looked so completely insignificant that I simply can't describe his face. But I do know that he had a grey herring-bone cloak, and he laid a grey hat on the table. Still, if you were to parade ten or a dozen men in front of me, I am quite sure I couldn't pick out the detective. But if you were to parade a thousand I could pick out the other man. I think it would simplify matters if you were to ring up the Schöneberg detective bureau and ask if they sent anyone to call on me. If so, he would come straight to the Gestapo. Then you could dictate his description yourself."

Again there was a smile.

I stood up, saying, "Is that all now? Oh, dear! I ought not to have given you such exact details. I have really done an abominable thing. I am sorry now that I told you."

The secretary bowed to me. "You are a good German!"

All my life I have told the truth. Not on religious principles, or on moral grounds, but simply because I thought it beneath my dignity to lie; I preferred to accept half responsibility for my actions. Now I was compelled to lie. And I found that I was able to lie most beautifully. I never felt the slightest conscientious scruples. I was acting in self-defence against criminals, and it was a positive satisfaction to see them swallow my lies.

I gave the matter much thought, and I even consulted a friendly pastor. He was a man for whom I felt admiration, for despite his religious and pacifistic views he had a true warrior's heart.

"Of course I tell lies," he assured me, "when I have dealings with the Gestapo. How else is one to protect oneself against these criminals? But, of course, I do it with a bad conscience."

"What am I to do if I am required to take an oath?"

"It is naturally your duty to commit perjury if by so doing you can rescue a human being from the talons of these monsters."

Yes, one has to lie in the Third Reich.

The Nazis lie to the people, in order to make them compliant, and in order to excuse their crimes.

We, their enemies, lie on ethical grounds and in self-defence.

The lukewarm lie out of cowardice or for the sake of convenience.

Can we wonder that the morale of the German people is undermined, seeing that it has lost all ethical standards?

Last Meeting

ON THE DAY AFTER MY EXAMINATION by the Gestapo the postman brought me a package. It came from the administration of the Dachau camp. It contained the few modest possessions which Hans had been able to preserve on his removal to Dachau: brush and comb, a pencil, a small photograph of myself, and sewing materials. Not a line from Hans.

I cried aloud: "He is dead!"

They tried to reassure me. But there was no other explanation. Then, on turning out the box, we found a note from the bureau: "Enclosed are the articles which the prisoner does not require on his discharge." There was still a faint ray of hope. Had he perhaps been released? Was he perhaps on the way to us? But my feelings told me that he was dead. I was incapable of lucid thought. Heinz rang up Dr. Berndorfer, telling him the facts, but without mentioning the enclosed note. I was lying unconscious, and he must know what had really happened, so that he could reassure me.

"Is my brother dead?" he asked.

Dr. Berndorfer: "No, I have no knowledge of his death."

Heinz: "I suppose that deaths are not so frequent in Dachau that you would not be informed of it?"

Dr. Berndorfer: "There is no reason to assume that he is dead. I should certainly know it if he were."

Heinz: "Won't you be so kind as to get into communication with Dachau immediately?"

Dr. Berndorfer: "I can't do that."

Heinz: "Then I must do so. Will you kindly tell me the number of the camp?"

Dr. Berndorfer: "I have not the least idea how one gets into communication with Dachau."

Neither had Heinz, but he rang up the "Feramt," and was actually put through to Dachau. He asked for the man who had signed his name as the sender of the parcel. When he was asked what the despatch of the parcel meant, he explained, quite pleasantly: "Well, you know, we're so full now, and there's so little room, no one can keep any extra stuff."

Heinz: "But you enclosed a note, from which I understand that my brother has been released."

The man: "Perhaps that isn't correctly expressed. He hasn't been released. But if he should be released he won't need the things."

It seemed fairly certain from this conversation that Hans was alive.

Some ten days later I at last received the promised

permit, with the remark that the Führer had granted me the privilege, as before, of paying a visit once every quarter. I was therefore in favour as an informer!

On the following day I went to Dachau.

Heinz accompanied me, since after all this excitement I had had an attack of syncope.

On arriving in Munich we immediately inquired at the official travel bureau as to the connection with the Dachau concentration camp. We were told, very rudely, that this connection was no concern of theirs. A private travel bureau informed us—but very politely—that it had no knowledge of any connection. No one ever inquired about it nowadays. Nothing was known by the hotel people either, but they promised to do their best; we should certainly receive some information during the day. And after a while an employee of the hotel appeared, who gave us some advice as to the journey.

After I had gone to bed there was a gentle knock on the door of Heinz's room. The same employee appeared again. "Is your Frau Mama already asleep?" he whispered. "She mustn't hear me. But I must warn you. The conditions there are terrible. If she sees or notices anything there she mustn't express any indignation. She must behave as though she noticed nothing, or they'll arrest her at once."

He began to execrate the conditions obtaining at the camp, and the Government as well; and Heinz replied:

"What did you people expect? After all, it began here in Munich, in the Bürgerbräu!"

"What do *we* expect? Sir, you are libelling us: it was you foreigners, you Prussians, who mixed the broth for us!"

We left for Dachau at eight o'clock next morning. At the place where the omnibus stopped we made inquiries of several people. They all turned pale when they heard the word "camp." No decent people ever went there, they assured us. Even a man with a party badge in his buttonhole exclaimed, indignantly: "Since 1933 I don't want to have anything more to do with Dachau."

Was there an inn anywhere near it? asked Heinz. He would have to escort me to Dachau and wait outside for an hour. And it was raining. No, there was no inn anywhere in the neighbourhood. "But for God's sake," he was warned, "you mustn't wait near the camp! Anyone loafing about there will be locked up immediately!"

From Dachau village it is quite a long drive to the camp, which is in a very isolated position. The whole place is surrounded with a high wall, on the top of which is a barbed wire fence. It is like a small fortified city. A long, wide street runs through the middle of it, and on either side of this are long, low, barrack-like buildings, which look like the temporary premises of an exhibition.

I had to wait an hour, as the commandant was absent, and without his personal permission no one was allowed to enter the camp. At last the permission came, and I was escorted down the long street to a small office. It was like a street of the dead. I saw only one prisoner; he was cleaning a window, and an armed sentry was standing beside him.

Just before we reached the office a cart came towards us; it was loaded with all sorts of provisions, and was being pushed and pulled by about a dozen prisoners. They were pale and woebegone, and they were wearing all sorts of badges—red, blue and green armlets. I do not know what these meant. They all stared at me as though I had been a most improbable apparition, and the guard who accompanied me yelled at them: "What are you staring at? Eyes front!" After that none dared to raise his eyes.

In the office a man in civilian clothes, who was sitting at a desk, recited all the rules which I must observe. I had been accustomed to this at the other camps; but here the rules were much stricter. To begin with, I was forbidden any physical contact with my son. There would be a wide table between us.

"Hitherto," I said, "I have always been allowed to kiss my son on my arrival and when I bid him goodbye. Why can't I do so here?"

"Of course, I can understand," he said, "that a mother would wish to kiss her son when she hasn't seen him for a long time. It isn't that we are heartless: but it offers an opportunity of communicating with the prisoner."

There was the usual prohibition: I must not mention the camp in any way; our conversation must be perfectly intelligible; and on the slightest infringement of these rules the interview would be terminated.

"Is your son a Jew?" he asked.

I recited our family pedigree.

Hans, apparently, did not know that I was forbidden to kiss him. When he approached me I called out, "Please stay where you are, at the other side of the table. Our usual greeting is not allowed here."

His eyes seemed to say: "You see already how different it is here!"

We sat facing each other, at either end of the table, which was six feet in length, and so high that I could see little more than his head and shoulders. The guard sat between us, at a separate table, so that he was nearer to each of us than we to each other, and he made notes of our conversation. It was impossible to whisper a single word, or even to make a sign. All I could see of Hans was a very thin, unhappy face, with very weary, mournful eyes. He was tanned, so I concluded that he was working in the open. Unfortunately I could not see his hands; they were hidden by the table. I could see only that he now and then pressed one of his hands, automatically, to his heart. This meant that his heart was in bad shape again.

He was wearing a very shabby, tattered field-grey uniform, with red stripes sewn upon it, and on each of the stripes was a round spot.

I inquired after his health. He looked as though he were in pain. The question seemed to alarm him, and he said, in a toneless voice, that he was very well.

His voice was strangely quiet, and without resonance. Only once or twice did a little life come into it. When I remembered his vivacity, his interest in everything, his joy at seeing me on my other visits, it seemed to me that he was a different person. Our conversation had always been so lively; but now we did not know how to begin. There were things of such dreadful importance to be said —and we could not say them.

"Of course, you were expecting my visit," I said.

"No!" he replied.

"But why not? Didn't you get my letter?"

"Yes; you said you would be coming. But I didn't believe it."

"But I wrote to you saying that I had permission from the Reichsführer himself. After that, you couldn't doubt that I should come."

"No, you didn't tell me that."

We exchanged a startled, inquiring glance. We both understood, at that moment, that my letter had been withheld because our correspondence was suspect. This was the letter containing the reference to "the valiant Swabian Stauf."

"Did you get my last letter?" asked Hans.

"No; but then I had just left home. No doubt I shall find it on my return."

Another anxious silence.

I told him then that I could again come to see him once a quarter; the Reichsführer had given me permission. I told him what I had written in the suppressed letter, though in different words. I said there was going to be an agitation on his behalf; and I asked him for his critical opinion of the theme of a film in which Heinz was working.—"Yes," he said, "I agree; I think it's an effective subject." This meant: "Yes, do your utmost!" And then he said: "I don't think the content of the Anglo-Saxon manuscript of which you wrote is historically true. I believe the novel of which I read a review has elaborated the actual facts." This meant that he did not believe that he would be released, as I had written, but rather that he would soon be dead.

I asked what he was reading. Formerly I had been allowed to arrange for a newspaper to be sent to him; he was free to choose the paper. Recently only the extreme party organs, such as the *Völkischer Beobachter* and *Der Angriff* could be received; they were ordered through the camp, and I had to send the money for them to Hans. For some weeks now he had not been getting the money. I wanted to find out whether he had received any newspapers.

"We both read the *Völkischer Beobachter* now," I

said. "When I read it I often wonder whether you are reading the same lines."

He did not reply to this; so I knew that he was no longer receiving any newspapers.

"How are you keeping up your reading now that you haven't your books?" I asked. "I suppose you have a camp library here?"

He answered, reluctantly: "Yes, yes, when I've time."

This meant either that they had no leisure, or that they were not allowed to read, even in their so-called hours of recreation.

But here the guard interrupted me: "Frau Litten, you know that you are not allowed to send any books here. What did you ask just now?"

"No," I replied, "I wasn't going to send any books"; and I changed the subject.

I told Hans all sorts of anecdotes about his friends' children, in whom he was still keenly interested, in spite of his misery; and in this way I managed to make all sorts of consoling remarks. For example, I told him that Margot's youngest child, Elnis, had developed a passion for singing; he had appointed himself choir-master to a troop of his friends, and had made them practise his favourite song until they nearly dropped. What was the song? "Verzage nicht, Du Häuflein klein"![1]—His sister, Birute, was a precocious little thing. She was taken to see a film in which Shirley Temple was the heroine, and

[1] "Don't lose heart, little thing!"—Tr.

now, in season and out, she was always quoting the line: "A year of sorrow is only a drop in the ocean of joy." Hans understood these consoling remarks, even if he had not any faith in them. The warder did not understand them; I told these little anecdotes with a great deal of expression; the important words were spoken with very little emphasis, while my description of the zealous choir-master, Elnis, and his harassed choir was so lively that the warder missed the point.

When we bade each other goodbye we kissed our hands to each other, and my son gazed at me with an infinitely loving and melancholy smile. *He* knew that we should never meet again.

I thanked the warder, saying: "I hope I haven't done anything amiss, but there is something I should like to ask you, since the conditions here are so terribly strict. What happens if one breaks the rules—for example, if one writes a line too much?"

"That all depends," he said. "If it's a purely formal violation you get the letter back. If you write anything objectionable the letter is added to the prisoner's dossier."

I knew now what had become of my last letter.

Heinz had been waiting for me in the car. This, according to the chauffeur, was the safest place. He at once gave me a sign to indicate that I must not speak of Hans or get into conversation with the chauffeur. He told me afterwards that he had tried to question the chauffeur, and on the first pretext the man had burst into a panegyric. What a fine man Commandant Boritz was, and what splendid fellows the SS men were! Some of them were friends of his. And what a pleasant life the prisoners led! Oh, one could be sure of that!

At home I found that the letter of which Hans had spoken had not arrived. So that two had been intercepted. I decided that I must warn Hans. I wrote him three lines on a postcard (ten were allowed), saying that I had been so delighted to see him again, and would write at length as soon as I had received the letter of which we had spoken. This card was returned to me, stamped with the word "Zurück." I could not understand why.

I went to see Captain Suchannek and showed him the postcard.

"Can you see anything objectionable in this card?"

"No."

"Can you tell me why it has been returned to me?"

"No."

"Then what am I to do? I find that both our last letters have been intercepted. And in order to get something through I write this short, inoffensive postcard, and it comes back to me."

"You must apply to Dr. Berndorfer; the affairs of the camp are in his charge. I expect he can explain the matter. By the way, when you visited the camp, were you satisfied with your son's condition?"

"I didn't see any traces of maltreatment."

Suchannek was evidently relieved. "There, you see how needlessly you worried yourself; you see that everything is all right."

"I haven't finished," I said. "I saw no marks of illtreatment. But I saw only my son's head, and that at some little distance. He looked very wretched; he was absolutely apathetic; he gave me the impression of a man who has not long to live."

"Oh, you exaggerate. After all, it's quite natural that a man who has been five years in camp shouldn't be particularly lively and pleased with things."

"In these five years," I said, "I have seen my son in a great many different situations. I know just what it means when he is so dull and apathetic. And there is something I want to ask you about. My son's uniform is not marked any longer with the plain red stripes that indicate a political prisoner: there is now a large yellow spot on each of these stripes, and also on his chest and his legs."

"I don't know anything about the uniform worn in the camps," replied Suchannek. "I can't tell you what that means."

"I suppose you know what the yellow spot meant in the Middle Ages?"

"No," he replied, "I haven't a notion."

"The yellow spot," I said, "is the badge of the Jew. They have brought that out again, and put it on the uniforms of the prisoners in the Jewish company. I have seen it already on some of the people in Lichtenburg. How is it that my son is suddenly wearing the yellow spot, which he has never had placed on his uniform before?"

"I know absolutely nothing about these things," replied Suchannek. "You must apply to Dr. Berndorfer."

And as I was going he said: "Then you will be reassured now that you have seen no traces of ill-treatment."

My conversation with Dr. Berndorfer was almost the same, word for word, with the difference that he referred me to the camp commandant, adding: "But you will write very politely and amiably, won't you?"

So I wrote very amiably and politely to the camp commandant.

CHAPTER IV

"For Publishing Reports of Atrocities . . ."

Dachau, 23rd November, 1937.

For publishing reports of atrocities in connection with the Dachau concentration camp through the Jews abroad we are isolated here and can send or receive no letters until further notice.

HANS LITTEN.

Was that the answer to my letter?

I felt that an attempt was being made to lure me into a trap. That our correspondence was regarded as suspect was obvious from the fact that our last two letters had been suppressed. Perhaps they wanted to see whether this fact would be reported in the foreign Press. If it were, they would have me in their power. So I must find out whether other such cards had been written.

Heinz, having obtained the address of the relatives of a half-Jewish prisoner in the same company as Hans, found that he had written a similar card.

In the meantime I received another communication from Hans:

Dachau, 6.12.37.

The *Neue Vorwärts* (Karlsbad) No. 229, date 31.10.37, the *Deutsche Volkszeitung* (Paris), No. 46, Vol. II, date 19.11.37, the *Deutsche Volkszeitung* (Prague), No. 44, date 31.10.37, and *Die Stimme*, Jewish newspaper (Vienna), No. 693, date 10.11.37, have once more published atrocity lies about the concentration camps. These shameless lies are invented by the emigrant Jews. The Jews in Dachau are again under suspicion of having smuggled lying news to them out of the concentration camp. Until the culprits are known we Jews are placed in separate confinement.

We inform you hereby that for the duration of such isolation we are strictly segregated, lose all comforts, and can neither send nor receive letters.

It is for you to persuade the emigrant Jews in Prague to tell no more such senseless lies about the concentration camps in future, since the Jews in Dachau, as their racial brethren, will be made responsible for them.

Hans Litten.

After this challenge I could take action.

I rang up Dr. Berndorfer, read the above letter over the telephone, and said that I would of course take the steps required of me, but I should like to consult him first. He replied that he had absolutely no time to spare on the following day, as he would have to hurry from conference to conference. I did not need his advice: I had only to do as I thought fit. When I persisted he said: "Please apply to my representative, Herr König."

And he immediately fixed up an appointment for me. He apparently had the intelligence to see that this affair might involve him in all sorts of unpleasantness, which he was anxious to avoid.

My letter must be so worded that the newspapers would be warned of the terrible conditions in Dachau, and would therefore continue their campaign. On the other hand, the letter must give the Gestapo the impression that I was anxious to stop the reports of atrocities.

I called on Herr König, explained why I had come to see him, and submitted my plan of writing to the emigrant Press.

"Yes," he said, "I think that is quite all right. But after all, it's a simple matter: why do you need my advice? You just write: 'I beg to inform you that I have seen my son, and that I found him in good health and spirits.'"

"No," I said, "I don't think that would be effective. I know, of course, that this statement is expected of me, and I am going to make it, in order to stop the atrocity propaganda. But there is one thing that I should like to say at once: I can solemnly assure you that I did not find my son in good health and spirits; on the contrary, I thought he was in a really terrible state, and I must once again insist that he should be treated differently. I don't want to offend you by saying these things, just when I am asking for your advice, but they must be said officially, or otherwise, if I make any further complaint, you might say to me: What on earth do you want? After you had visited the camp you made a public statement to the effect that you found your son in good health and spirits. So as far as I can see nothing would be gained by such a statement.

"I am extremely anxious to stop these reports of atrocities in the foreign Press, in order to save my son and the other prisoners from this horrible situation. But if I simply write what has been suggested these people won't realize what terrible harm their articles are doing the prisoners. Besides, they'll say: Of course, she's an old woman; she's stupid; she doesn't notice anything. And they may even say: 'She's an Aryan; naturally she's lying!' "

König was horrified. "How can you say that an Aryan woman is naturally a liar?"

"You are always saying that the Jews are liars. So it follows as a matter of course that the Jews will assume that the Aryans are liars."

He gazed at me very thoughtfully. I continued: "I have written a letter already, saying what I think I ought to say, but I should like to submit it for approval."

"Really, Frau Litten," he said, "you can do just as you like. You must realize that we have nothing to say in the matter."

"Yes," I said, "I know that. But one never knows what the effect of one's actions will be. And I have no practice in such things. I really don't care to write without the approval of the Gestapo. I don't want to be told afterwards that I have behaved deceitfully. If you approve of my letter I shall know that everything's all right."

I showed him the draft of the letter which I should have preferred to send. This is what I had written to the four émigré newspapers:

"My son writes to me as follows"—and then came a copy of his letter.

But Herr König objected to this. "No, of course you can't send a copy of the letter."

"But why?" I asked. "Why on earth not? Then these people will know precisely what is happening; they will draw their own conclusions, and keep silence. And that's all that matters."

"No," he said. "In this letter all the newspapers which have published atrocity stories are mentioned. I really don't think it would do to send that."

So I submitted my second draft, saying: "I don't really like this as well. It's a good thing I brought it. Perhaps you will think it better." Strangely enough, he had no fault to find with it. This letter ran as follows:

4th December, 1937.

To the Editor of the *Neue Vorwärts*, Karlsbad.

On account of your issue of the 31st October, 1937, the Jewish prisoners in Dachau concentration camp are suspected of having smuggled lying news out of the camp.

Accordingly the Jews in Dachau concentration camp are placed in separate confinement until the guilty persons have been discovered. They informed their relatives on the 27th November, 1937, that during the period of isolation they are strictly segregated, and are deprived of all comforts, and also that they can neither send nor receive letters. They have written to their relatives: "It is incumbent on you to persuade the Jews to refrain from telling such senseless lies about the concentration camps in future, since the Jews in Dachau, as members of the Jewish race, are being held responsible for them."

I hereby declare that on the 25th November, 1937, I was allowed to visit my son in Dachau and found him in good health and spirits. My son assured me that all is well with him. I beg you will influence the above-mentioned emigrant circles, with which I have no connection of any kind, in the sense which my son desires.

IRMGARD LITTEN, née WÜST.

When König had approved of this letter, while assuring me yet again that he really had not wished to see it, that he had read it only because I insisted that I must have his advice, and that I could naturally do exactly as I pleased, I said: "All the same, I should be very greatly obliged if you would mark this with the Gestapo stamp."

This was going too far. "No; one really can't do that sort of thing. Whatever put such an idea into your head?"

"I was afraid that without the Gestapo stamp my letter would never cross the frontier. You see, I am writing to four newspapers which are apparently given to publishing the most dreadful stories of atrocities; and I am writing about the camp. Such a letter would certainly be stopped at the frontier."

"No, no!" he said. "Arrangements have already been made to pass it."

That was too much for me; I stared at him in perplexity.

"Well, yes," he said. "The authorities in Dachau apparently wanted you to write, so I assume they will see to it that the letters go through. By the way, would you mind leaving this letter here? I expect you have a copy."

"Of course," I said. "I would much rather that you should know exactly what I have written."

During this interview I made one more reference to the Jewish question. I told König: "I must once more express my indignation that my son should be placed in the Jewish company. Not because I think it dishonouring; in this matter I absolutely repudiate the views of the Third Reich. I object to it for quite other reasons: namely, because I know that in all the camps, and especially in Dachau, the Jewish company is shockingly ill-treated."

I explained that my son should not properly have been placed in the Jewish company. It was a flat violation of the law, and I should make an appeal to the Reichsführer if the Gestapo could do nothing about it.

"That wouldn't be much use," said König. "I can

tell you beforehand what the Herr Reichsführer would reply: the Gestapo is above the law. And the Gestapo has decided that in the camp a man is a Jew if he had only 25 per cent—indeed, if he has a single drop—of Jewish blood."

Finally, he told me that I must always come to him if I needed his advice. He would be at my disposal at any time.

I wrote the approved letter on the typewriter, with several carbon copies, and sent only the carbons to the newspapers. This made it plain to the editors that it was a circular letter—though they would have understood this from my prefatory remarks.

I registered the letters, paying for certificates of receipt, and the punctual arrival of the receipts told me that they had been delivered.

By chance we received a Prague newspaper, printed in the German language, whose headlines ran:

"Himmler's Blackmailing Letter to the D.V.Z.

"The Mother of the Rechtsanwalt Litten compelled to Sign."

Under this was a photograph of my letter, and the whole case of Hans Litten, with all its horrors, was once more given publicity. The letter had produced a much greater effect than we had anticipated.

Not until eighteen months later was I able to discover some of my son's fellow-prisoners in Dachau, who were able to tell me of the conditions there during the period of isolation. It was not easy, for many of these men were still so terrorized by their experiences that they were afraid to speak of them even to their closest friends. They had been told that any relatives of theirs who were still living in Germany would be subjected to the most frightful punishment if they ever spoke of their experiences as prisoners; indeed they were told that there was no part of the earth's surface, however remote, where the arm of the Gestapo would not reach them if they should speak. Others were still suffering so acutely from the shock of their experiences that their one and only desire was to forget them. They were unwilling to recall them deliberately.

But from the report of certain young prisoners who knew Hans well in Dachau I was able to compile the following account:

Hans was confined to No. 6 barrack, in which there were then about 180 men: Jews, half-Jews, quarter-Jews. There were young men who had been shifting about the world; homesickness had brought them back to Germany, and now they had been brought to Dachau for "re-education." There were "race-defilers" too; even old men of seventy had been imprisoned for the crime of "race-defilement." Among these somewhat uninteresting and uninterested men of the lower middle class were some twenty "politicals," and a few artists and intellectuals. These quickly formed themselves into a little community. Most of them were familiar with my son's professional record; others had heard of the terrible things which he had suffered, and his kindness to his fellow-prisoners; for prisoners were so often transferred from one camp to another that they all had knowledge of things which had happened in other camps.

No. 6 barrack had an admirable "elder," the twenty-five-year old student, Heinz Eschen, from Munich. A young Communist, he was a distinct personality, and a man of the highest principles. As a rule, the most brutal elements were appointed as elders, foremen, and so forth. Since they were punished for any infractions of the regulations, and were responsible for the work done by the prisoners, it was not surprising that these originally bad characters soon learned to torment the prisoners even more brutally than the SS men. Even the comparatively decent prisoners quickly became brutalized when they were appointed to such posts. This was simply a matter of self-preservation. They were naturally venal, and prisoners who could give them money were better treated than the rest. And so not only brutality, but every kind of corruption and espionage flourished. A prisoner must have a strong character if he was to remain a decent human being in such an atmosphere. Many succumbed to temptation, turning informers in order to secure better treatment.

The kind of "examination" which followed any denunciation in Dachau, and indeed the most trivial incident, was as far as I knew an innovation. The prisoners' wrists and ankles were tied together behind their backs, and they were suspended in this condition, their weight falling on their bound wrists and ankles. Or their hands were bound behind them and hauled up until their feet left the ground—and so they were kept until they "confessed."

Have we the right to reproach a man if after hours of such torture he says what is required of him? Is it not indeed comprehensible that he would swear that black was white in order to escape such "questioning"? There were heroic prisoners who were steadfast for hours. Heinz Eschen, the day before Hans' death, hung for nine hours from a tree without "confessing." Next day he was found in the cellar—hanged.

Life in camp was like life in the rest of Germany in this respect: the authorities did their utmost to break men's spirits, to kill every moral sense, every trace of humanity. The purpose was the same: but in camp the means applied were more brutal. If the attempt was unsuccessful in the case of many of the prisoners, this was simply because the men confined in the concentration camps and the prisoners are, for the most part, the salt of the German people.

Why should the Government seek by all possible means to pervert and corrupt and ruin the German people? Because a nation which shivers with dread, a nation degraded to the level of a horde of cowardly slaves or brutish criminals, which has lost all sense of human dignity, all sense of right and wrong, will be incapable of rising in its wrath against a government of bestial gangsters. One can persuade such a people of anything, can use it for any purpose. It will be ready for any atrocity which its rulers may require of it.

The political prisoners stood by one another more steadfastly than the others; they had, as a rule, more backbone. Their principles kept them straight.

Heinz Eschen and his circle, seeing that Hans was terribly depressed, and extremely unhappy in his new environment, did their utmost to cheer him up. Eschen and Hans became close friends.

In Buchenwald my son had had another accident. The fact that he had a stiff leg was not taken into consideration; apparently he had been run over again, and his injured leg was once more broken. Every step was agony, but he had to do the same outdoor work as a hale and hearty prisoner. The sight of his sufferings was so distressing to his comrades that they would not let him do any work indoors; but out of doors, under the eyes of the guards, always waiting to kick any prisoner who was not working quickly enough, it was impossible to help him.

On the 24th November an order was issued which was no novelty to the Dachau veterans. The Jewish company was isolated!

One of my son's friends told me:

The windows were screwed fast and whitewashed; the doors locked. We had to make copies of a note and send them to our friends abroad. We wrote these letters willingly, because we hoped that they would for the first time really call the attention of the outer world to the terrible state of affairs in Dachau.

I do not know if it is possible to convey the atmosphere of an "isolation" to an outsider. The air is nauseating. The strawbags lie so close on the floor that there is no room to move about. I have already described the sort of men with whom one had to live. Thefts of bread began. One had to spend the whole day doing nothing on the strawbags, which lay close together (three men to every two bags), without a book, without a newspaper, without a pencil. Quarrels were constantly occurring on the slightest pretext, and in this overcharged atmosphere they soon degenerated into fights.

We politicals had almost all of us formed ourselves into a group. We made a very different use of our enforced leisure; we tried to elucidate all manner of different problems that interested us.

Hitherto we had helped Hans Litten, so far as it was possible, on every opportunity. Now he became the central point of our group.

One day he was given permission to see his mother. He came back from the interview a different man; he was quieter, and he looked more contented. The "block-leader," who had been present at the interview, had already expressed his astonishment, in his Bavarian idiom, that the Littens should have talked about art or "fiddle-faddle" of that sort.

Hans, whose views on art were in many ways different from ours, discussed them with us during the isolation period. Among us was a well-known expert in the history of literature. Even he declared that he had never met a man with such a wealth of knowledge. In order to substantiate his opinions on artistic matters he constantly quoted Rilke, six days in succession, the discussions continuing for four hours at a time. But he dealt with other matters also. His plan for the day, during our isolation, was more or less as follows: as soon as we had risen and swallowed our gruel Hans would begin a discussion with some of us, dealing with the history of German literature from the first beginnings. In the course of these discussions he would as a matter of course quote pages of the authors in question, though he had never made any notes. Afterwards, until dinner-time, he discussed history with other comrades. Whatever his subject, he supported his individual opinions with such convincing evidence that one could hardly refute them.

In the afternoon he listened to a comrade who gave a series of lectures on psychology. In the evening he would sometimes tell us something of his legal experiences.

All this he did so simply, and with such good breeding, that even if one were intellectually his adversary one could not help liking him.

He had formerly been rather quiet and depressed, but he came to life again during the period of isolation. In his own peculiar way he tried to divert and interest us all, for he set up as a psychoanalytical interpreter of dreams.

But we could not be deceived as to the state of his health. He would sometimes collapse completely, and suffered from long fainting-fits.

Despite our persuasion, he would not spare himself. His greatest satisfaction was to be of use to us, to give us something. In the evening, when we sang our songs, his face would grow rigid. One felt that he was recalling his childhood. Very often, late in the evening, he would relate some amusing incident of his travels.

Intended as a martyrdom, for us politicals isolation was a season of relaxation. What did we care for the carbon dioxide, the stench, the quarrels of our fellow-prisoners?

Hans recovered his spirits during this period. The sense of firm solidarity gave him strength.

The period of isolation continued until after Christmas. No Christmas parcels could be sent—no Christmas greetings.

At the beginning of January it was briefly intimated that the barrack would be opened. I realized from his letters that the state of affairs was still appalling, and that Hans believed that his death would not be long delayed.

I could do nothing, beyond asking my foreign friends to begin a strenuous agitation. One could no longer consider whether this would endanger Hans. It was now simply a question of preventing his murder by appealing to public opinion throughout the world.

In England, however, the rumour was current that a comprehensive amnesty would be granted in January. It was hoped that Hans would benefit by this, and it was thought that any agitation on his behalf might irritate the Government.

As by the end of January no amnesty had been granted, our friends decided to begin a great fight for my son's life. An article which Lord Allen, to open the campaign, had written for *The Times*, reached the Press when it was too late. . . .

CHAPTER V

I Meet My Son's Murderers

ON THE 5TH FEBRUARY a police officer brought my husband the news of my son's death. The news had been telephoned from the camp; my son had hanged himself. If we wished, his body would be sent to us. My husband did not dare to tell me the truth; he rang up Heinz, asking him to come home. I happened by accident to overhear his part of the dialogue, and I guessed at once, from my husband's condition, the nature of the news which he had received.

We knew that the body would be sent to us in a soldered coffin, so that it would not be possible to ascertain the cause of death.

I rang up the Gestapo, asked for Captain Suchannek, and said:

"Heil Hitler! I have just received the news that my son has hanged himself in the Dachau camp. I wish at all costs to see the body, and I beg you to give me the permit immediately. Heil Hitler!"

Even over the telephone I could tell that Captain Suchannek was taken aback. "I knew absolutely nothing of this," he declared. "Excuse me—I must make inquiries first. I will ring up again."

Half an hour later Captain Suchannek stammered his nicely worded condolence, saying that he had telephoned to Dachau: I should be allowed to see the body, and he would not put me to the trouble of coming to fetch my permit; he himself would give the necessary orders to Dachau.

A friend of mine, a woman doctor, declared that she would not allow me to go without a medical attendant; she would come with me herself. I did not want her to run into danger, but she replied: "What could happen to me if I accompany a sick woman as her doctor?"

I had not known her very long, but I knew that when human beings were in distress she was always to the fore, helpful and efficient.

We took the night train to Munich. Early the next morning I rang up the camp, and was told, in reply, that I could come at once. We drove to Dachau immediately. I, of course, knew the way. At the entrance-gates it was evident that the guards had been notified of our arrival; I was admitted without more ado once I had given my name. In consideration of my state of health the doctor was allowed to accompany me.

In the courtyard I was received by a fat little man in SS uniform. His chest was covered with ribbons and medals. He introduced himself as Baranowski, and was addressed by the two men in mufti who accompanied him as "Herr Kommandant." These two civilians were introduced to me as doctors, and one of them was described as the first person to see my son after his death. This man had a terrible, criminal face; he looked the typical murderer, the sort of person who might figure on the cover of a cheap detective-story.

It was strange that this man should be a doctor. I should have taken him rather for a torturer. The other man did give me the impression that he was a doctor. Herr Baranowski, who had greeted me by shaking my hand quite amiably, made a few condoling remarks; he was very sorry for what had happened, and if he had had any suspicion of my son's intentions he would have kept a better watch over him.

"But," he continued, "I really could not have expected such a thing; on the very day before his death your son seemed perfectly calm when I questioned him a little."

I was roused by this. "Questioned him? Then I know everything; I know your questionings. My son has already attempted suicide after such an examination."

"No, no!" he said. "Don't distress yourself. It wasn't the sort of questioning that you mean. It did not concern your son personally at all. He was only asked to give me some information about a few of his young comrades who had behaved foolishly during the isolation."

"In plain German," I said, "he was asked to inform against his comrades. And he took his life because he knew what was in store for him if he did not inform against them. He had been through that also once before."

"No, no!" said the Commandant. "We parted on quite friendly terms. I even had a conversation with him about the ancient Greeks and Romans. Your son, of course, was a highly educated man."

I could not reply to him in that tone. I was so bursting with rage that I could not discuss the matter any longer. This uneducated lout dared to make patronizing comments on my son's education! He repeated several times that my son had told a fellow-prisoner, one of his more intimate friends, that he was going to take his life before the end of February.

In reply to my questioning he declared that my son had hanged himself. At ten minutes before midnight; in the latrine.

"How do you know the time so correctly?" I cried.

"He was found very soon after that," the commandant explained, "and one can tell approximately when death occurred."

"Did my son leave any farewell letter for me?"

"No, only a note in which he said that he had taken his own life. The only other thing on him was your last letter."

Why did he write this note? It was impossible that any of his comrades could have been suspected of murdering him. And he certainly would not have been at any pains to exculpate his deadly enemies, the SS men, for they were his real murderers, whether they had killed him themselves or had driven him to take his own life by their devilish tortures.

"I want that note, please."

"I can't give it to you; it has been filed with his dossier."

"Then take it out for a moment and show it to me."

"No, that is impossible."

Why was it impossible? It would certainly have been expedient to show me the note if it really existed.

We were taken into the morgue. It was a very small, smoothly plastered room, apparently built for this purpose. My son was lying in a very narrow deal coffin, stained brown and smoothly finished; really a box, which had apparently been put together by his comrades. He was tightly swathed to the chin in a white linen shroud, so that I could see only his head. It was an austere, emaciated head; haggard, but the features wore a certain expression of relief. I thought: "St. Francis must have looked like that." His lips and the back of his head were white as snow.

The ordeal of being confronted with the body of a hanged man had filled me with unspeakable dread. In my childhood I had once found a dead man hanging in the forest, and all my life I had remembered the bloated face, the starting eyes, the protruding tongue. There was nothing of the sort to be seen here; only a noble and wonderfully beautiful head. The coffin stood rather high above the floor. I went to the head, and my friend tried to follow me, but the two male doctors immediately took her between them—though without using force—and placed her at the foot of the coffin.

My first thought, when I saw the tightly swathed corpse of my son, was to throw myself upon him and in so doing push aside the carefully adjusted shroud. But this was impossible; the coffin stood too high. But I *would* know the truth. And I determined, even at the risk of immediate arrest, that I would quite deliberately tear away the white wrapping. At this moment I felt on both my arms the light pressure of the commandant's hands. I knew that if I made the slightest movement he would seize me, and that I could not carry out my intention. I must abandon the attempt as futile.

I was allowed to stand there quietly as long as I wished. I knew that I was standing with his murderers beside the corpse of my son. I knew that they were waiting for the moment to seize me. I did not move, though I was shaking with despair and the wildest thoughts of vengeance. But I knew that the slightest movement would prevent me for ever from carrying out my plans of reprisal.

Shall I ever be able to do what I vowed to my son in that moment? Suddenly it seemed to me that he was smiling faintly; and strangely enough, my friend had the same impression, as she told me afterwards. I began to speak to him, very quietly and cautiously; I was afraid that he would not understand me if I were silent. My friend was afraid that I should commit some imprudence; she made a sign to the commandant, meaning that he should interrupt me. But he did not move. My conversation with my son, like all my intercourse with him during the last five years, was camouflaged, and apparently so successfully disguised that the others did not grasp its meaning. . . . I began to stagger slightly, and we went out into the open air.

The commandant thought I was looking ill; he advised me to lie down for a few minutes in the doctor's consulting-room. It was next door to the morgue; the two rooms apparently constituted the whole of the hospital quarter. When I sat down, hemmed in by these people, who never took their eyes off me, my friend took a flask of medicine from her bag and handed it to the man with the criminal's face, saying, in a quick, imperious tone: "Colleague, twenty drops!" I was not quite so weak as I looked. I noticed how the man picked up a glass; he evidently did not know what to do with the phial. This was curious, in a doctor! And so the other doctor seemed to think. He snatched the phial away from him, left the room for a moment, and returned, saying: "She can have the drops." He numbered the drops himself and handed me the glass. Were they by any chance afraid that I was going to act the tragi-comedy of an unsuccessful attempt at suicide?

I stood up in order to discuss a few formalities. I received permission to bury my son's body. In respect of the necessary formalities I must apply to the Gestapo in Munich.

I wanted to get the body away from Dachau as quickly as possible. But it was Sunday, and until the following day I could not get into touch with either the Gestapo or the undertakers. I thought all this could be done on Monday morning, and asked permission to send for the coffin early on Monday. The commandant replied: "It won't be possible to hold the funeral before Tuesday. We are allowed to send bodies out of the camp only during the night."

They saw me off the premises very politely, standing in a row beside the car as I got into it, and remaining with their arms raised in the rigid Hitler salute until I had driven away. This time I really could not bring myself to reply to the salute. I had often enough done so, gritting my teeth the while, in the camps and at the Gestapo. It would do Hans no harm now if I failed to give the salute. I drove off without giving it, sitting stiffly erect.

CHAPTER VI

Matthew Passion

NEXT MORNING I promptly attended to the distressing preparations for the funeral. The hotel employees were kind and helpful; they remembered me from my former visit to Dachau.

The young man who had gone to Heinz in the night now came up to me cautiously, when for a moment I was alone in the writing-room, and inquired after my son. He was almost beside himself with rage when he heard what had happened. He declared that there had been innumerable suicides among the prisoners; and he warned me to be extraordinarily careful; very few Nazis —thank God!—came to their hotel, but one could never be sure that there wasn't a spy in the place. The hotel employees were safe, but the guests were not. And while I was in the hotel I must not seem to know him apart from the rest of the staff, or he himself would be watched and endangered.

My first errand that morning was to the Gestapo. The man on duty at the entrance door was apparently expecting me, for when he heard my name he directed me immediately to the proper man. The official whom I saw there was extremely polite; he was anxious to save me trouble, and offered to deal directly with the municipal burial society. I told him that I would rather leave everything to the crematorium to which all the members of my family were subscribers (of course, with the exception of my eldest son). Very good: he would ring up the crematorium. They could send for the body at once.

"That won't do," I said. "The commandant informed me that the bodies of prisoners can be handed over only at night."

The official was evidently annoyed and embarrassed: "But what nonsense! No, there must be some misunderstanding!"

He made all arrangements with the undertakers, but just as I had taken leave of him the company rang up again to say that they were very sorry, but they could not undertake *this* commission. So we had, after all, to apply to the municipal burial society. I had to interview a woman employee in order to arrange the details of the ceremony. She was surprised when she heard my requirements.

"The very cheapest funeral?" she asked.

"Yes." It seemed a mockery to bury my son with any sort of pomp or display.

"But do you know that means no trees in the hall, no decorations and no music?"

"Yes, yes, I know. And I should like my son to remain in the simple wooden box in which he was coffined in Dachau."

But I meant to fetch him. I ordered a hearse with accommodation for mourners.

"No, there's no such thing in Munich."

"Then I shall want a car as well. As regards fetching the body, money is no object; I don't want anything to be third-rate there."

She looked at me inquiringly for a moment; then she said, very quietly: "Will you allow me to give you some advice? It isn't the custom in these parts for the relatives to drive in a car following the hearse. It would attract a great deal of attention, and I'm afraid you might have to put up with a lot of unpleasantness."

I thanked her, and said that I would take her advice. I had only wished to show the authorities at the camp that I did not hesitate to pay the customary marks of respect to the dead.

Then we went to the crematorium. The people there were nice and polite to me; though they looked rather astonished when I mentioned the simple form of the ceremony, and suggested that it would seem very bare and simple.

"I don't want my son to go to his grave otherwise than as he lived."

"A clergyman?"

"No!" I said, emphatically. "I wouldn't on any account have a clergyman.   (I was afraid of falling into the hands of a 'German Christian.')   But I should like to have good music."

"Good music?   But good heavens, they won't play much on the organ at so cheap a funeral!"

"It doesn't matter in the least what the music costs. But I shall want certain pieces of music."

They sent for the organist, and I told him I wanted a certain piece from the Matthew Passion music.

Oh, but they never had that in a funeral programme. That really wasn't possible!

"It means a great deal to me," I said.   "I so very much want the passage: 'Then all the disciples forsook him and fled.'   It is when Christ is taken prisoner and all draw away from him in dread."

"Couldn't it be a similar piece of music?   I could easily find something."

"I am very anxious to have precisely this music," I said. "Not long ago I was speaking of this passage to my son. He was working on a translation of *Der Heiland*, and he explained how he was expressing the mood of this scene by a certain manipulation of the metre.   He thought the poet, in *Der Heiland*, had been trying to do just what Bach, eight hundred years later, did in music, in bringing out the spirit of this scene."

The organist looked at me for a long while; then at last he said: "Of course it can be done.   I have the whole night before me. I hope you will be content with the music."

In the afternoon I took flowers to the crematorium. The coffin was not there. I had to go then, because the gates were about to be locked. I sat for an hour outside the churchyard gate, until the gatekeeper told me that it would be useless to wait any longer; no more coffins would be brought in that day.

So the official at the Gestapo was wrong; there had been no "misunderstanding"! No: *the bodies of prisoners were sent out only at night!*

Next morning, as we were approaching the crematorium, a pastor came out of a house near by, and, having accosted me, he said a few very kind and consoling words. He had been a great admirer of my son; he had followed his fate with great sympathy; and innumerable Germans felt as he did.

In the hall of the crematorium I found that the coffin had already been placed upon the bier, and covered with a beautiful pall. My flowers were lying upon it. The room was richly decorated with green plants, and behind the coffin stood a huge, bare wooden cross, which in its stern simplicity filled the room with an indescribable atmosphere of solemnity.

It was strange: they had told me that everything would be so bare and dreary if I chose the simplest form of funeral. And they had told me, too, that if I would not have a clergyman present the room would be strictly un-ecclesiastical.   And now this tremendous cross gave the room the air of an Early Christian chapel.   How strange, that in this Catholic region there should be a bare cross, and not a crucifix!   I learned afterwards that it was the cross which was employed at the funeral of fallen soldiers.

The organ sounded; it played the chosen passage from the Passion music.   It was beautifully executed, and followed by a long series of variations.

There was no one in the room excepting my friend, the woman doctor, and myself.   I had made sure beforehand that no camp or Gestapo official would desecrate the ceremony by his presence.

I knelt before the coffin until it sank into the depths.

EPILOGUE

By Pierre van Paassen

ALTHOUGH THE NAZI movement has in our day come to be regarded by many (not only in Germany) as a god-send, it cannot be said to have dropped from heaven as a ready-made instrument for the destruction of those liberal-democratic institutions which we in the West have inherited from the nineteenth century. Nazi Fascism could embark upon what now looks to be its predestined task in the world—namely, that of preventing, or at least postponing for a time, the fruition and the fulfilment of democracy—only after it had won its spurs, after it had gained approval, after it had invented and set forth a social doctrine that would answer to the economic interests of a certain class in society, and, above all, after it had proved itself of a more serious character than a conspiracy of congenital crackpots and military putschists.

The small group of Adolf Hitler's first disciples was scarcely calculated to win the confidence or even to attract the notice of the German bourgeoisie. It was made up of the Viennese housepainter himself, the little man who began ranting in a violent and almost incoherent manner whenever he saw before him what looked like an audience; an ex-aviator, Goering by name, who had fallen on evil days and whose family had vainly tried to cure him of addiction to narcotics by a period of confinement in a Swedish asylum for the insane; the young litterateur Joseph Goebbels, turned from a pronounced philo-Semitism to bitter Jew-hatred after the Berlin critics had dismissed his first novel as so much trash; an unemployed schoolteacher named Feder, who was an admirer of Mussolini; another individual streaked with a queer twist, Moeller van den Bruck, who died insane; a notorious vehme-murderer, Captain Roehm; and a few others who showed equally small promise of statesmanship in the land of *Dichter* and *Denker*.

For a brief moment that strange company did nevertheless manage to reach the footlights. That was in 1923, when General Erich Ludendorff, the bitter and frustrated military genius, joined with them in an insurrectionary move. But the plotters did not stand up under the whiff of grapeshot which Ebert's troops sent in the direction of their ridiculous barricade. Ludendorff donned false whiskers and a pair of colored glasses, and fled to Sweden. Goering followed. Adolf Hitler, who had flattened himself on the ground at the first shot, was arrested with Hess, Roehm, and the others. They were tried, and were sentenced to amazingly light terms of imprisonment. The general belief in Germany was that they were a crew of harmless fanatics whom a short spell behind the bars would sober up effectively and thereafter disperse forever. With the Munich beer-hall Putsch the Nazi adventure seemed to have come to an end. The appeal of its discredited leaders, made chiefly on the note of Jew-hatred, had been without noticeable effect on a people which had been taught by August Bebel that anti-Semitism is the socialism of damn fools.

In the leisure and comfort of their prison cells the conspirators concocted a new doctrine. They realized that what unified the ruling classes of Germany and those of the victorious Allied countries was their fear of Bolshevism. They learned, through the publication of the state documents from the secret archives of Berlin and Moscow, that Germany might have avoided the great humiliation of Versailles had the Wilhelmian Reich volunteered to lead a crusade against the East instead of temporizing with the Bolsheviks in the days following its military defeat. They learned, moreover, from the memorandum which General Sir William Robertson, British chief of staff, had forwarded to Lloyd George in 1916, that England's aim after the war would be to build up a strong Germany, in pursuance of her age-old balance of power policy and to offset the hegemony in Europe which would obviously fall to France. Hitler and his friends drew their conclusions from these data: they constituted themselves into an anti-Bolshevist movement *par excellence*.

By setting themselves up as the most determined opponents of Marxism they at once gained the sympathy and the support of that considerable section of the petty bourgeoisie which takes the bogey of Socialist confiscation as a real threat to its unstable property values. German big business hesitated to throw its support to the Nazis as long as Hitler had not given a guarantee that control of industry and finances would not pass into the hands of the party. Prompted by Franz von Papen, who assured the liaison between German and French armament trusts in the days of the Weimar Republic, the Fuehrer finally gave that promise, therewith assuring himself of the Nazi party's rise to power. For from that moment Hitler had, besides the backing of the Thyssens, the Froweins, and the Stinneses at home, the support of the industrial and financial oligarchy in France in his efforts to make the continued existence of the democratic republic in Germany impossible. From the late twenties onward the supreme hope of the international banking and steel cartels was vested in the person of Adolf Hitler. He had made no secret of it that his chief plan, once he should have attained power, was to attack Russia and turn that country's vast and rich domains into colonies for German exploitation.

In order to carry that project into effect the rearmament of the Reich was pre-essential. But the rearmament of Germany was also the condition *sine qua non* of a general rearmament campaign. In giving Hitler carte *blanche*, the masters of Europe, who were the leaders of big business in France, figured on killing two birds with one stone: to eliminate the hated Bolshevik regime in Russia, which had subtracted one sixth of the world's surface from capitalist exploitation, and at the same time to utilize the artificial rise of Hitler's power to whip up nationalist-chauvinist sentiment at home in order to stimulate the armament business. The financial contributions of French capitalists and steel trusts, like the Schneider-Creuzot armament firm, to the Nazi party's exchequer constituted pump-priming with a vengeance.

Hitler reached his goal in the beginning of 1933. Without a moment's delay he set out to prove that the confidence imposed in him at home and abroad would not be betrayed. He crushed the labor organizations, muzzled the press, dissolved parliament, squelched freedom of conscience, forced the churches into a straitjacket, proscribed learning, regimented youth—in a word, he eradicated democratic institutions in Germany root and branch.

Still his regime was beyond criticism in the France of Laval, Flandin, and Bonnet, and in the England of Chamberlain, Simon, and Nevile Henderson, that ambassador whose mission to bring about a harmonious cooperation between Britain and Germany failed. It failed not because he could not bear the sight and the knowledge of the human degradation that went on all around him in the Reich—Henderson was full of praise for Hitler's social achievements even, as he specifically states in a recent book, after the introduction of the Nuremberg Laws—but because Hitler broke his word after Munich: Instead of marching East, as he had promised, he clashed with British imperialist interests. For years Chamberlain and Baldwin and Simon were impatient in the House of Commons with critics of Hitler's methods. They silenced the indignation over the Nazi murder regime with the cynical falsehood that what the Chancellor-Fuehrer did at home was of no concern to free-born Englishmen, that protests would be interpreted as interference in the private affairs of a nation with whose rulers His Majesty's Government was on terms of friendship.

How often, too, did we not hear an expression of regret in Holland and in Belgium and in France, before the invasion of those countries, that there was not a Hitler at the helm to deal with democratic incompetence and waste and labor-coddling, as had been done in Germany?

It is precisely because of this attitude of laissez-faire and half-concealed admiration that the Nazi regime has gone from strength to strength, has conquered virtually all Europe and now girds its loins for the final struggle against the Western hemisphere. For it would be a distortion of the truth if I did not say with all the conviction at my command that Germany plans the conquest of the

United States of America after she has Europe securely under her thumb.

When the soldiers in Hitler's assault cars, rumbling into the old European capitals of Prague and Warsaw, Oslo, Amsterdam and Brussels, sang *"Heute gehoert uns Europa und morgen die ganze Welt"* [Today Europe is ours, and tomorrow the whole world], this was no mere soldiers' ditty inspired by a momentary exaltation over victories speedily won. Those words echoed the fundamental ambition and sheer, unbreakable determination of Germany's leaders and braintrusters, her scientists, philosophers and chiefs of the general staff, from the time of Otto von Bismarck to the latter days of Adolf Hitler.

On the plan-maps and economic charts openly published in Germany the conquest of this hemisphere appears today as a foregone conclusion. The territory of the United States is already shaded in the German color, the same color that covers the national territories of Czechoslovakia, western Poland, Scandinavia, the Low Countries and the north of France. On those charts the British Isles are a mere outlying province of the Greater German Reich; there are located the main shipyards that are hammering together the new merchant marine with which the Reich intends to carry on its trade with its trans-Atlantic and trans-Pacific possessions. America is shown as the chief German market, where industries are allowed to operate only in so far as they do not compete with German home industry. However, neither the control of a single industry in America nor the direction of any important phase of American national life is to be left in the hands of native Americans. Everything is to be administered by trusted Nazi commissioners sent over here from the Reich.

If no direct attempt has been made by Germany so far to seize the wealth and the markets of the American continent by force, this is not because such a seemingly fantastic enterprise is considered beyond feasibility or beyond the Reich's power. German strategists in fact look upon the conquest of the Americas as a relatively easy job once they are in a position to deal directly with American defenses. Germany will never need to worry about the United States, promised Dr. Hans Delbrueck, one of the fathers of the Pan-German expansionist policy which the Nazis are carrying out. "It is extremely questionable," he wrote, "that under prevailing laws, political conditions, and extraordinarily easy changes from one party to another, the United States will be in a position to attain to a permanent military status at all. Their momentary proud position should not deceive any one. The Americans have not yet stood any severe test." America is no military factor with which one needs to reckon, he concludes.

Modern military experts in the Reich speak of the defenses and the fighting forces of the United States with the utmost contempt. Economic Counsellor Hugo Schmidt of Stuttgart, who is an adviser of Germany's marine staff on submarine warfare, dismissed the possibility of effective American aid to the Western democracies with the words: "I never worry about America. It does not amount to anything." Marshal Goering, too, when confronted with the news that the Allies were acquiring large quantities of fighting planes in this country, shrugged his shoulders and said: "What difference does it make? America does not frighten us in the least. We will have won the war before America can make a single effective move."

Speaking to the present writer in 1931 on Hitler's intention of taking up where Imperial Germany had left off in 1918 in its plans of world conquest, Herr Goering laughed heartily when the objection was made that he would probably find the United States on Britain's side once more. "*Ich denke nicht daran,*" he shouted. "I waste no thought on it. *Die Amerikaner sind ja nur ahnungslose Leute,* naïve, absolutely unsuspecting people whom we can fool more easily than any other nation. We will defeat Britain in the next war before the Americans realize that their only protection is gone." He referred to the British Navy.

No, it is not fear of America's fighting power that has deterred the Germans so far from making an attempt to conquer this hemisphere. The project has required infinite preparation, careful preliminary maneuvering, vast and painstaking labor in both the diplomatic and the military field, study of American psychology and a careful watching of economic trends in this part of the world and elsewhere. What has held up the staggering scheme, which was on the point of being launched at least twice in the last seventy-five years, once during the Civil War and once during the Spanish-American War, is what the braintrusters of the German military machine call the absence of a propitious *Konjunktur*, a term that denotes a favorable combination of circumstances of a military, economic, and even of a psychological nature. The time was hitherto not ripe for the masterstroke of history. The plot to conquer the Western hemisphere from Labrador to Tierra del Fuego, which if successfully carried out will make Germany the undisputed mistress of the world, was worth delaying until preparations should be completed in the smallest detail.

With the coming to power of Adolf Hitler that favorable *Konjunktur* for which the Reich has patiently and uninterruptedly been waiting and planning, through good times and bad, through war and peace and inflation and civil strife, is now taking shape and becoming ominously visible. The war in Europe is the last colossal effort to clear the road for the supreme task which Germany has set herself. If the Reich emerges victorious from the struggle with Great Britain, the final objective of her world planners lies clear and naked before her.

Germany's military leaders consider the war against

the European nations unleashed by Hitler in September, 1939, a mere preliminary test of strength, a limbering up, a gaining of experience for greater military exploits to come, for the titanic duel of the continents. Once Europe has been brought completely under German domination, the vanquished nations, with all their resources and equipment, industrial plants and shipyards, oil wells and steel mills, munitions and poison-gas factories and bacteriological laboratories, are to be welded into one single, unified, continent-wide war economy for the conquest of the rest of the world, beginning with the Western hemisphere.

These plans are set forth in painstaking detail in the published works of Professor Karl Haushofer of Munich, who is also a general in the German army and the scientist who has done the thinking for Hitler so far. He is the head of the braintrust which has worked out the details for the successful campaigns in Europe and steered the Fuehrer in the perpetration of the greatest mystification of all time: his veering about as soon as he had the precious Sudeten fortifications in his possession, when, instead of marching East against the Soviet Union, as he had screamingly announced on every possible occasion that he would do, he turned Westward instead and fooled everybody.

It is not by armed might alone that the European nations were conquered. They went down before a double onslaught of steel and of betrayal, intrigue and double-crossing. They were thrown into hopeless confusion. Their own radio stations, suddenly overpowered by Fifth Columnists, blared Hitler's lies. Troops were sent in the wrong direction. Secret plans of the general staff were stolen by spies, necessitating not only revision of campaign strategy after attacks had begun but also a change in the supreme military leadership in a most critical hour, as in the case of Gamelin and Weygand. Instead of the armed forces finding the enemy in front of them, bands of traitors stabbed the defenders in the back. Within a few hours a situation of chaos was created, making all resistance appear senseless and hopeless. Entire nations were overpowered before their armies could take up their defense positions.

Throughout the German war literature of the last fifty years runs a note of regret and anger over the fact that Germany did not succeed or even make an attempt at obtaining a footing in the Western hemisphere in the days when Spain, Holland, England, and Portugal carved colonial empires for themselves out of this continent. Thus General von Bernhardi and Heinrich von Treitschke, two of the most prominent leaders of the imperialist expansionist school, ask why Germany did not at least secure a foothold somewhere in America, either in the North or in the South, to serve as a basis for the protection of her interests and for gradual penetration. They cite the opportunities of striking a blow for the German empire which had presented themselves, and not only they but many of the strategists and economic technicians make it clear that the victory of the North over the South, that is to say, the preservation of the Union, was the heaviest setback German territorial aspirations in this hemisphere could have suffered. Germany should have supported the South in the Civil War, they argue, not because of the righteousness of the South's cause or for any other sentimental reason, but because that might have led to the establishment of two rival nations on this continent, one of which would have been under German influence and would have provided the jumping-off place for the total subjugation of the Americas.

According to Professor Francisco Bulnes, Mexican engineer and scientific thinker, in his book *The Whole Truth about Mexico*, Germany has publicly declared that she does not recognize nor will she ever recognize the Monroe Doctrine. It is practically certain, says Professor Bulnes, that if the European war of 1914 had not taken up her attention, Germany, because of her great interests in Brazil and her designs in Nicaragua, would have declared war against the United States—if, he adds, she could have secured the neutrality of England.

Writing in 1916, Professor Bulnes goes on to say: "If Germany crushes the power of England in the present war, she will, with a reconstructed navy, attack the United States, not only for the purpose of destroying the Monroe Doctrine, but for the purpose of breaking a rival power. Rome would not have stood the rival power of

Carthage in the twentieth century any more than she stood it two thousand and seventy-two years ago. The cause of the Allies is the cause of the United States, and explains the unprecedented interest and support given on supposedly neutral ground to Germany's enemies."

It is unquestionably true that the archives of the State Department at Washington abound with documents which prove conclusively that the possibility of an invasion of the United States was envisaged by Germany long before its air and sea fleet came into existence. As a matter of fact, the first great German navy, which was built from the year 1887 onward, was intended primarily to abolish the Monroe Doctrine and prepare the way for a German penetration of the Americas. It became known, for instance, that the German navy was being built to assist Spain in her forthcoming war with the United States, and American Ambassadors in various European countries warned the then Secretary of State of the danger the new German naval weapon presented to the United States.

If at that time, in 1887, the danger of a German attack was realized by the American Government—that is, at a time when the British navy still lay between Europe and this country and America could have formed several protective alliances with European countries—one wonders why the present danger is being sneered at. For now there looms an almost almighty Germany, a Nazi-unified Europe with all the resources of Europe at its command!

The skeptical military and political leaders and the molders of public opinion in our country, who seek to minimize the actual danger to this country and wave away all warnings as alarmist hallucinations of warmongers, might read with good profit some of the works of General Karl Haushofer and study the maps which illustrate those ponderous books. It might surprise them—if they are not altogether blind—that as there are maps and charts showing the conquest of the European lands which have already passed under the German heel, so there are detailed charts showing the military and naval bases which Germany actually has in South America and the centers of concentration of the Fifth Column, within the territory of the United States, on which the Reich relies for cooperation at the right time.

Hitler has time and again given proof that these books, charts, and maps of his Geopolitical Institute are no idle academic speculations. But he knows that the most effective way of disarming American public opinion is to publish these plans openly and make them available in public libraries. In one of Haushofer's major works, called "The Geopolitics of the Pacific Ocean," which sold three editions in the Reich and which may still be obtained in German bookstores in New York and Chicago, there are charts showing the spheres of interest into which Germany and Japan plan to divide "the land of the free and the home of the brave."

It is all done so openly and brazenly that one still hesitates to take the matter seriously, in spite of the realistic lesson that the world ought to have learned from the cataclysmic events in Europe. The very brazenness of parading these plans and maps under our eyes is apparently the best method of lulling to sleep a people's alertness and suspicions. For there is calculation in this seemingly naïve frankness. The first reaction of any normal person at the sight of a map showing his country under foreign domination is to say that it must be the work of crackpots and deluded megalomaniacs, and that if Germany were really serious about the conquest of Holland or Scandinavia she would not be so foolish as to give the game away by publishing in advance into what administrative districts the German military would divide the land following its subjugation.

We forget that the lie is the Nazi power's strongest weapon, that Hitler declared himself the most faithful disciple Machiavelli ever had and that consequently any weapon—no matter how contemptible or base, whether intrigue or betrayal or poison, in natural form or in the shape of propaganda—is utilizable and is utilized by a regime which is, by its own confession, the declared foe and antithesis of Christianity and the civilized virtues. And so it even uses the truth deceitfully.

What is not realized in this country, except by a few students of geopolitics whose words have hitherto fallen on deaf ears, is that events in Europe are but the first phase of the coming gigantic war of continents which the German general staff has planned no less minutely than it planned and executed the subjugation of the better part of Europe. Just as inevitable as an irresistible onslaught on the British Isles following the invasion of the Low Countries, so inescapable is the attack on the United States once Europe has been unified under a Nazi military dictatorship.

The execution of the first part of Germany's world program, the unification of Europe, has advanced so far that early in May Adolf Hitler appointed Hjalmar Schacht, the former President of the Reichsbank, and a financial wizard, as the head of a select commission of financial and economic experts to study practical means of putting the European union plan into effect. In May Hitler and his advisers considered the conquest of Europe no longer a theory but a virtually accomplished achievement. The second phase of the plan, the welding of Europe into a single economy, could be taken up while the armies dealt with the scattered resistance of France and England.

But the gentlemen from Missouri still want to be shown. They have not seen enough. They still insist that what has happened in Europe does not in any way concern the safety of this country. They are playing most perfectly the role of the *ahnungslose Amerikaner*, of naïve Americans, which Hitler has assigned to them, and act the part of "idiotic Yankees," a title which Franz von Papen bestowed on those who shrug their shoulders while Germany acts.

The great and unforgivable mistake of the democracies is that—although Hitler and his predecessors and collaborators had at no time made a secret of their projects of world conquest, while they in fact spoke of them openly and wrote of them in detail in unmistakable language in books and newspapers that were scattered in the tens of millions of copies—the German plans were not taken seriously until the mechanized armies battered down the gateways of the guardhouse of freedom in Holland, thus opening the road to Paris and London.

In some quarters Hitler was dismissed as a megalomaniac. Reams upon reams of paper were filled with statistics and irrefutable evidence that Hitler was incapable of waging a war on a large scale for any length of time. The lack of oil, experts insisted, would halt the Nazi war machine almost before it would get started. Other so-called reliable sources spread the word that a powerful underground political movement in the Reich would bring about the fall of Hitler as soon as his soldiers set foot on foreign soil. Whispering campaigns sprang up from mysterious sources, telling the world that the German high command would never stand for the ex-paperhanger in wartime. Now we know that much of this anti-Hitler propaganda was skilfully disseminated by the Fuehrer's efficient espionage system, with the collaboration of Fifth Columns everywhere.

While Hitler armed and virtually announced the time schedule for his European war there were still democratic countries where it was made a crime to say or write a word of evil against that head of a friendly foreign State. Impartial investigators who came back from the Reich with irrefutable stories about the Nazis' diabolical schemes to blast populations of entire cities to death were branded as sensationalists. Newspaper correspondents and political observers, non-Leftists and others, who warned that the bombing of Barcelona was merely a try-out for the total war against England and France, were denounced as hirelings of Moscow. Persons who tried to point out that the persecutions of the Jews in Germany were merely forerunners of an attack on democracy and the Christian Church were disqualified as hysterical old women. Even when Hitler announced his lightning war against the West a roar of incredulous laughter went up about the Blitzkrieg that did not blitz.

Then, when public opinion was lulled to sleep and men and women were firmly convinced that Hitler's bark was worse than his bite, he struck—and civilization reeled under the impact of the blow.

www.ingramcontent.com/pod-product-compliance
Lightning Source LLC
Chambersburg PA
CBHW071920150726
47999CB00001B/56